Freight Broker Business Startup

The Complete Guide to Start, Manage & Grow a Successful Freight Brokerage Business From Scratch

Darryl Gates

Text Copyright © [Darryl Gates]

All rights reserved. No part of this guide may be reproduced in any form without permission in writing from the publisher except in the case of brief quotations embodied in critical articles or reviews.

Legal & Disclaimer

The information contained in this book and its contents is not designed to replace or take the place of any form of medical or professional advice; and is not meant to replace the need for independent medical, financial, legal or other professional advice or services, as may be required. The content and information in this book has been provided for educational and entertainment purposes only.

The content and information contained in this book has been compiled from sources deemed reliable, and it is accurate to the best of the Author's knowledge, information and belief. However, the Author cannot guarantee its accuracy and validity and cannot be held liable for any errors and/or omissions. Further, changes are periodically made to this book as and when needed. Where appropriate and/or necessary, you must consult a professional (including but not limited to your doctor, attorney, financial advisor or such other professional advisor) before using any of the suggested remedies, techniques, or information in this book.

Upon using the contents and information contained in this book, you agree to hold harmless the Author from and against any damages, costs, and expenses, including any legal fees potentially resulting from the application of any of the information provided by this book. This disclaimer applies to any loss, damages or injury caused by the use and application, whether directly or indirectly, of any advice or information presented, whether for breach of contract, tort, negligence, personal injury, criminal intent, or under any other cause of action.

You agree to accept all risks of using the information presented inside this book.

You agree that by continuing to read this book, where appropriate and/or necessary, you shall consult a professional (including but not limited to your doctor, attorney, or financial advisor or such other advisor as needed) before using any of the suggested remedies, techniques, or information in this book.

Table of Contents

Introduction

Chapter 1 : A quick background of the Fright Broking Industry

Chapter 2: What is a Freight Broker

Chapter 3: Freight brokers, Forwarders and agents

    Freight Brokers

    Freight Agents

    Freight Forwarders

Chapter 4: History of Freight Broker Business

Chapter 5: How to become a Freight Broker

    An Independent Career

    More Time for Important Things

    Better Income

    No Commute

    Low Start-Up Costs

    Low Overhead Expenses

    Unlimited Earning Potential

    Growing Business

    A Family Business

    A Family Legacy

Chapter 6: How to find your first Fright broking customers

Chapter 7: Tips to running a Successful Freight Brokerage

Chapter 8: Licensing and Business Registration

Chapter 9: Obtaining Freight: Brokers vs. Direct Shippers

Chapter 10: How to Get the Best Drivers

Chapter 11: Determine the Best Area of Operation

Chapter 12: Analyze Your Competition

Chapter 13: Important Gear and Tools

Chapter 14: How to Scale Your Business

Chapter 15: What to Expect in the First Two Years

Chapter 16: Secret Tips to Increase Profit of Your Trucking Business

Chapter 17: Office Personnel: Safety Coordinator, Broker, Salesperson & Dispatcher

Chapter 18: Inspection and Maintenance

Chapter 19 : Promoting and Marketing your Freight Broker Business

Conclusion

Introduction

In the broader transport sectors, a variety of people who need shipping like business owners, distributors, and suppliers of goods and services sign contracts with trucking companies to transport goods to intended destinations. However, there is still a significant quantity of freight that is managed by freight brokers. Truck brokering aims to maximize the profits acquired through freight hauling as they facilitate lucrative cargo hauling interactions between freight companies and trucking firms.

Who is a Freight Broker?

A freight broker is an expert who acts as the mediator between a trucker and carrier with the capacity and ability to move cargo that needs transporting.

The Need for Freight Brokerage Services

As mentioned, goods are transported by transport companies that have a contract agreement with freight companies. However, there are numerous instances where cargo needs shipping but no trucks are available. Consider this: a trucker receives a call for a huge amount of cargo. Unfortunately, all their trucks have already departed to various destinations. If taken care of, huge amount of income can be made for this additional load to be transported. In such instances, freight brokers come in handy.

How to Make Money as a Truck or Freight Broker

A registered freight or truck broker builds relationships with trucking companies to easily handle moving freight cargo. If your truck company runs out of available vehicles for shipping, the broker would lease the additional cargo to another transporter and then receive a small commission in the process.

As a general rule, trucking companies often negotiate their own cargo. If they have an insufficient number of trucks, they lose the chance of transporting the additional cargo as well as the opportunity to broker the new shipment to another transport firm.

Opportunities Abound in the Freight and Tracking Sector

To be completely honest, it is a great time to become a freight broker these days.

With the continuing evolution of technology and the internet age, the opportunities for any interested individual to start their own brokerage business grows.

In the past couple of years, the US economy improved significantly. With it comes the growth and expansion of the logistics and transport industry, therefore, an increased demand for freight brokers.

Generally, A Freight Brokerage business has strong potential profit-wise. All experts in the transport and logistics industry agree that now is the perfect time to begin a freight brokering company, with a possible income of at least $90,000 a year. Also, freight brokerage companies are indispensable in the goods and cargo transport industry. Basically, such firms keep the industry going. If you are reading this with an interest of learning how to begin your own freight brokerage firm, read away and begin to work as soon as possible.

Starting your own Truck Brokering Business

Before starting any business, it is advisable to learn as much about the industry as possible. For instance, what does trucking involve? What are the licensing or registration requirements? You need, of course, clear answers to all of these questions before you begin. You will also need to understand what the role of a freight broker is within the broader transport industry.

Compliance

One of the most crucial aspects of the truck brokerage business is compliance. As with all industries, there are rules, regulations, and requirements. If you learn how to comply with these rules, then you will get off to a great start.

Procedures such as late renewal penalties, bond claims, and consumer complaints that can deplete your money and time can be avoided by keeping yourself informed and secure. Complying with regulations is extremely important as the truck broker industry grows again. The number of freight brokers has been growing each year steadily by about 1,000 per year since 2014. At the start of 2015, there were slightly over 15,000 licensed freight brokers in the US. This figure rose to slightly above 16,000 in 2016, and in January of 2017, the number had grown to 17,012.

This steady growth over the last couple of years is due to one main reason: A steady increase in local freight volumes within the United States and also, an increase in export and import cargo. This steady increase in cargo business calls for more players in the sector, especially trucking brokers. Your efforts in choosing this path will help to move increasing freight volumes across the US and overseas.

Legal Requirements

Starting your own freight brokerage career is relatively straightforward. Like any other business, you will need to fulfill some legal requirements, especially getting bonded and acquisition of an operating license. If you are a new to the industry, ample training as well as direct industry experience. This will help you understand how to set up your business as well as all your legal obligations and requirements that will ensure you remain compliant.

It is important to acquire all the necessary information to guide you through the entire process. This book is precisely created to be an excellent resource for all aspiring trucking brokers.

Chapter 1 : A quick background of the Fright Broking Industry

The economy is experiencing a tremendous growth rate. This means that there is a big opportunity for smart people to launch their own successful businesses. One of the most profitable industries is trucking. The trucking industry is responsible for the movement of items across the country. It is a very competitive field. You might want to first learn as much as you can about the industry before you set up your own trucking company, or else you risk losing valuable time, energy, and money.

Most people tend to think that all trucking companies are similar, but that is not the case. You first need to decide precisely what role your company will fulfill.

Here are the main classifications of the trucking companies:

For-hire truckload carriers

These trucks essentially haul other companies' freight. Many companies need logistic support and supply chain management. Companies contract for-hire truckload carriers to transport their products. The business model is ever changing because it is based on the freight demands of the companies that you work with and contract terms. When the contract reaches maturity, the client – in this case the company – may allow other trucking companies to bid on it. And so, the nature and availability of freight are subject to change, and one of the measures of protecting yourself against loss is having multiple customers.

Private trucks

If you have a company that produces a particular product, you might want to distribute your own product as opposed to contracting out trucking companies. Private trucks are thus used to transport freight that belongs to the parent company. Whenever private fleets are unable to meet their freight demands, they may contract out other truck companies.

Household Movers

People are relocating every day, and they need to bring their stuff along. Establishing a household carrier company will facilitate the movement of peoples' belongings. Considering the high percentage of people who relocate because of family, financial or even work-related reasons, this is an especially lucrative field.

Inter-modal

In this model, the only function of trucks is carrying the freight to and from the railroad yard. This is how it works: a truck carries a load to the rail yard, the load is transported by rail, and finally, another truck carries off the load from the rail yard to its destination.

Market Research and Competitive Analysis

Market research will enhance the viability of your business, and competitive analysis will make your company stand out. Both market research and competitive analysis are important tools in ensuring the success of a company.

Market research is heavily based on studying economic trends and the behaviors of buyers. It gives you the ideas of product improvement in order to meet customer needs. These are some of the questions you may need to answer:

- Is there a demand for your service?
- What is the size of the market for your service?
- What are the financial abilities of your target customers?

- Where do your target customers live and can your business cater to their needs satisfactorily?

- Are there similar businesses operating within your target location?

- What is the best pricing for your service?

Draw Your Business Plan

Business plans help you start and run your company. They facilitate the structuring and growth of a business by allowing you to put down the key elements of your business. A good business plan will promote cooperation from important parties such as investors and managers. It will help you get funding or convince skilled people to work for you.

There are two main categories of business plans: traditional and lean start-up, but in both cases, the key elements of your business should stand out. The traditional business plan can be quite extensive, as it encourages pouring out the details in every section; while lean start-up business plans put emphasis on summarizing the key elements of your business.

Pick Your Business Location and Name

The location may determine the tax, laws, and regulations that your business will be under. So you have to select the state and city that aligns best with your business. On the subject of names, you should come up with something that is both catchy and professional.

Determine Your Business Structure

Your business structure might influence your tax dues, the ability to get funding, licensing, and liabilities. The best business structure finds a balance between legal protection and monetary gain.

Here are some of the common business structures:

Sole proprietorship

This structure gives you complete control of the business. In most cases, you are the sole financier and manager of business operations. One of the major downsides of this structure is the lack of separate business identities. Your personal assets and liabilities are not separated from your business liabilities and assets.

Partnership

In this structure, two or more people may own a business together. In limited partnerships, there is a general partner whose liability is unlimited; whereas other partners have limited liability. In limited liability partnerships, every partner enjoys limited liability.

Corporation

This is a business entity that is identified independently. The entity may be taxed and held liable. Corporations protect their owners from personal liability, but on the downside, they are expensive to establish.

Apply for Licenses and Permits

Businesses must obtain licenses and permits before operation from either/both state and federal agencies. The requirements for obtaining licenses and permits depend on the business location, activity, and law. Depending on your operations, here are some of the necessary permits and licenses for trucking companies:

- Form SS-4
- UCR Form
- Commercial Driver's License
- United States Department of Transportation Number
- Motor Carrier Operating Authority Number

- Insurance

Chapter 2: What is a Freight Broker

A freight broker is an individual or a company that connects shippers with authorized carriers. Freight brokers play a pivotal role in the trucking industry. They are well-connected with shippers, and as a new business owner, you may want to have good relationships with freight brokers so that they may send business your way.

Freight brokers are very resourceful and play a huge role in facilitating movement of cargos. They earn commissions by helping carriers connect with shippers and strike a deal to transport their loads. A shipper who doesn't have any connections with an authorized carrier contacts a freight broker, who in turn connects them with a reliable carrier.

Brokers can come from any background, but the key to success is being great at establishing relationships with shippers. A freight broker who has won the trust of regular shippers will have more orders than they can handle, but a freight broker who cannot create meaningful relationships with shippers usually ends up frustrated.

A freight broker may have an agent representing them, and the agent's work is similar to what a broker does, but the agent obviously represents the broker's interests. Experienced brokers have liability insurance that covers shipper's cargo in the event when the carrier's insurance fails. Brokers who provide insurance coverage are the best as it is indicative that they have a strong financial foundation and can offer quality services.

Over the years, I have noted that, even though broker agents work with various types of transportation, all of them essentially operate as the negotiator between a shipper with a consignment and a carrier, irrespective of whether the carrier is an airline, a railway, a motor carrier or any other means of transport. Despite these different modes of transportation, this report will focus on agents working in the trucking industry.

In an industry that is so vast and varied, a wide range of participants are required for it to flourish. Although some of the participants' titles may be a little unclear, and some of their duties may overlap, we will keep things as clear and simple as possible by looking at who the key players are and what they do.

There are a number of reasons why a company or consumer may choose to hire a freight forwarder rather than internally or personally arranging transport for their goods. Often the biggest reason for this is to get the best rate along with faster shipping for goods. A successful freight forwarder often has strong contacts within the shipping industry and is often aware of shipping options not available to the general public.

A typical event for a freight forwarder starts when they are contacted by a customer. Initially, information is gathered such as the merchandise being shipped if it has to cross international borders and other important issues (such as weight, size, perishable or nonperishable, hazardous or non-hazardous, etc.) regarding the shipment. Based on this information, the forwarder looks at all the shipping options available and gets the package to its destination on time and at a very competitive price.

Based on this it is easy to see how a freight forwarder can be confused with other similar jobs. The two most common jobs that a freight forwarder is often confused with includes freight broker and customs broker. Before we continue to consider freight forwarding, let's take a moment to see how a freight forwarder is different from these two jobs.

Chapter 3: Freight brokers, Forwarders and agents

The first thing you need to do before considering whether you want to be a freight broker is what distinguishes all the players in the logistics and transportation industry. The major jobs in this industry are freight brokers, freight forwarders, and freight agents. While these jobs may all look and sound the same, they are different in the tasks they do.

Freight Brokers

A freight broker can be a self-employed individual working full time from *home*. However, this can present the challenge of running an entire business while still finding the time to search for new shippers and carriers. A freight broker needs to run their business while also worrying about cash flow, billing and collections, marketing, networking and all the basic records keeping paperwork. This is where the job of a freight agent comes into play.

Freight Agents

Many freight brokers start their careers as freight agents. This allows those going into the freight industry to start at the ground level and recoup training investments while gaining the knowledge and hands-on experience needed to become a freight broker.

A freight agent doesn't need the authority licensing, surety bonds or insurances of a freight broker or freight brokerage business. The freight agent often works under the freight broker, so you don't have the financial pressure of running a business when you first start in the field. It also offers low start-up costs since you just need a computer, fax, and phone line from a home office.

The main responsibility for a freight agent is to find new customers and drivers. The majority of your time is spent on marketing of freight brokerage services, networking with shippers and carriers, doing reference or background checks, making sure loads get to their destination on time and troubleshoot load problems. Basically, a freight agent focuses more on the operational side of freight brokering rather than the strategic management side.

The benefits of this are that you don't have to worry about invoicing, billing, collections, cash flow, payroll or all the other financial grunt work that goes into running a freight brokering company. The negative is that as a freight agent you do have to share your commission earnings with the freight broker you are working for.

Freight Forwarders

A freight forwarder and freight broker may seem interchangeable to those new to the industry. The truth is there is some similarity between the two. However, after a little bit of time in the industry, you'll notice there is actually a considerable difference between these two jobs.

While a freight broker will often move commodities from shippers to carriers, freight forwarders are more likely to directly handle the goods that need to be transported. A freight forwarder transports cargoes and shipments internationally. This often requires them to receive smaller cargo and combine them into a larger shipment. This means a freight forwarder has to physically possess the goods, consolidate them and then determine the best shipping method whether it is land, air or water.

Because of the international component to a freight forwarders job; they often need additional knowledge, experience and licensing beyond the basics required by a domestic freight broker. A freight forwarder also needs to know customs including custom imposed duties, laws, procedures, and practices. Lastly, a freight forwarder may also need to be fluent in more than one language or employ people that are.

In my other book, "Freight Forwarder Business Startup" I explained the step by step process of becoming a freight forwarder, but I want to emphasize once again that it takes much more than just reading a book to become a freight forwarder or a freight broker. Though the process is much more involved and requires a lot more education and training for anyone to become a freight forwarder, than for someone to become a freight broker.

In my humble opinion, if you are interested in the logistics business, then I am sure you are already aware of the tremendous growth it has been seeing in last few years and especially with the growth of Amazon FBA business which has been growing at a phenomenal rate for last four years straight. Your best bet is to start out as domestic freight broker at first.

Start right from home, get your feet wet, make some connections, once you feel comfortable in the transportation arena, then grow out of your home to an office and hire some staff and eventually start your own freight forwarding company.

While there are many other jobs within the freight brokering industry, the main focus is on these three and defining them, so you know what you are getting into by becoming a freight broker. Now that we know the differences I want to take the time to tell you just why you should consider becoming a freight broker.

Chapter 4: History of Freight Broker Business

Little history lesson for you first. Before trucks and tractor trailers, freight was moved by train or a horse-drawn carriage for small, local shipments. Trains could only supply to the major cities and cargo then needed to be transferred by horse-drawn vehicles to smaller cities.

By the early 1900s, trucks were mostly a novelty. Most had engines powered by electricity so they couldn't travel far. Also, there were no paved roads in the country, so driving was difficult and often took hours or even days. This meant trucks were only used for small loads and short trips in urban locations.

Around 1910, new technological innovations created new opportunities for trucks. Perhaps the biggest change was the gasoline-powered engine. Second to this was the invention of the tractor and semi-trailer combo to help haul larger loads. This was when moving freight by truck started to increase in popularity. Still, rural areas had bad road conditions which lead to the trucks still being restricted to cities only.

During World War II, trains and railways became more congested, so trucks gained more exposure as the main method for hauling freight. This was when the government and shippers started to explore long-distance truck shipments as a solution. Pneumatic tires also help to offer faster speeds.

In the 1930s trucks were able to travel farther and reach new areas because of the addition of paved road networks. Then the interstate highway system was started in the 1960s to connect major cities and towns; something that wasn't possible before. This is when the trucking industry gained a foothold as a major transportation option and started becoming dominant in the freight industry. Trucking offers flexibility and agility over rail transportation.

Things were still complicated by the Motor Carrier Act passed in 1935 by Congress. The Interstate Commerce Commission (ICC) placed restrictive regulations preventing smaller players from entering the market easily. Industry stakeholders lobbied and deregulated the trucking industry in 1980, opening the sector to new players and a variety of configurations.

For example, warehousing companies started playing a larger role in freight shipping, and a lot of trucking companies started offering warehousing services. It also allows small businesses to start entering the logistics world, providing more competition to larger and more established companies.

As a result of this increase in service providers, the cost of shipping decreased (the rule of supply and demand). Shippers were finally able to shop around for the lowest price from the most reliable carriers. An increase in globalization and reduced trade barriers also allowed manufacturers to ship products further. This is the environment that allows freight brokers to begin and flourish. Manufacturers and small shippers that don't have their own traffic or shipping/logistics departments looked to freight brokers as a way to responsibly get their shipments delivered on time.

Even larger companies who had their own in-house logistics and supply departments were able to use freight brokers when their own departments couldn't handle their loads. Freight brokers helped to simplify the complex work of getting shipments to their destination by acting as a middleman between shippers and carriers.

Now that we've covered the background and start of freight brokers. Let's look at the modern freight industry and what a typical freight broker routine looks like.

Chapter 5: How to become a Freight Broker

Setting up your Home Office

When starting out as a freight broker, you really should start off with a home office. Not all businesses can be started from home; however, a freight brokerage firm can operate successfully from a home office. Many successful firms today started in basements and living rooms.

Setting up a home office is simple. You will need to designate a specific room within the home. You need to ensure that this room is set aside from the rest of the home, especially when you are working. For instance, you need to keep the kids away when you are working as well as pests or even guests.

Adopt a disciplined and official attitude when working so that others can let you work. No client wants to hear kids playing, dogs barking, or loud music when discussing business.

Essential Home Office Equipment

You will require specific equipment for your home office. If you already have basic pieces of furniture, such as an office desk and a comfortable, sturdy seat, then you are ready to get started.

1. Workstation

You will need a workstation in your home office. This is where you will primarily be working from. Get a large enough table or office desk as well as a high back chair. If you already have these at home, then you can use these as they will save you from buying new ones.

If you do not have an office desk and a high back chair, then you can easily find these being sold locally or online. You do not have to purchase the most expensive items on the market. Simply find a good quality, functional desk and chair and set these up as soon as you can.

2. Computer, Telephone, and Internet

You will spend most of your working hours on your workstation talking on the phone and using your computer. Therefore, get a dedicated office line instead of using the home phone line. This will set aside your private life from your work. It will not appear prudent for a client to call you only to speak to a family member.

Get a nice, modern, fast, and reliable computer for your work. A good computer is fast, has a large memory capacity and can handle large software programs and the various apps that you will need for your work.

Clear the Clutter

Make sure that your home office is devoid of any clutter such as knickknacks, old magazines, newspapers, and even electronics should be removed. These can easily cause a distraction and look unsightly. A cluttered space usually brings about a cluttered mind. However, if you have any items in mind that will motivate and inspire you, then you can add these to your office.

You should try as much as possible to be organized and stay that way. If you are organized, then you will be productive, creative, and efficient. However, if you are not organized, then you will be counterproductive and distracted. Distraction often comes from things such as incomplete tasks, loose papers, clutter, and so on.

To be organized, you should get a trash can, filing cabinet, and even a shredder for the office. These are simple items but will go a long way in getting you organized so that you are efficient in your work and can focus on delivering quality services to your clients. Some people are messy by nature, and that is easy to understand. If this is you, then it is okay to ask for assistance on how to stay organized.

Set your Office Hours

While standard office hours are between 9.00 am and 5.00 pm, you may want to experiment with your work hours. Since you are your own boss, then you are allowed to do this. A home-based job offers you the flexibility to choose your preferred hours. This way, you can create a balance between business and pleasure. You should create hours that suit you, and once these become agreeable with your schedule, you should share them with your family –it is important that they know when you are working and when you are free.

Make sure that you choose office hours when your body is rested and refreshed. You do not want to work when you are fatigued. Working when you are fresh ensures you are productive and can accomplish some of the most demanding tasks. Once you identify appropriate office hours, make sure that you stick to these.

Set up Business Savings and Checking Accounts

Keep personal and business finances separate. You may need to have both a savings and checking account for business. You also need to think about signing up for third-party payment processors, especially if you will be accepting credit card or online payments. You have plenty of options when it comes to bank accounts and payment options so shop around until you find something that you really like.

Get a Postal Address if Necessary

Sometimes you may need a postal address where you will receive all official communications. While this is not always necessary, it is a great option to think about. A postal address will get you to stand out as an organized broker and also an organized manager. You may choose to use the postal address for invoices, direct mailings, and company letterheads. This also allows you to keep your home or personal address separate from your business address.

Working from home has numerous advantages. You will have access to a standard office, but without the costs and overheads you would expect from a regular commercial office.

Bookkeeping and Accounting

You need to keep in mind that there are backroom issues involving your truck brokering business. These include invoicing, bookkeeping, payables, and invoicing. If you are new to the world of business and accounting, then you had better fold your sleeves and start learning.

While you do not really have to use accounting software, it makes a lot of sense to use it because it makes things easier. You can organize your finances properly and also manage your firm's accounts a whole lot better.

If you want to get your accounts managed professionally, then you will need to use accounting software. One of the best and most widely used is QBS or QuickBooks from Microsoft. QuickBooks is easy to use, readily available, and best suitable for all types of businesses.

When using QuickBooks, you will come across the three main categories:

- Classes
- Charts of Accounts
- Items List

These three main categories constitute the backbone of your freight brokerage business. Classes generate expenses and income. The charts of accounts and items list are very closely related. One points to your source of finances while the other seeks money from your clients.

The charts of accounts constitute a collection of categories that inform the government about your sources of finance and how you spent your money. On the other hand, the items list informs clients about exactly what you are billing them for. It indicates the kinds of services that you provide to them. These two items are linked together in your accounts.

Classes inform you how the income was generated. If you are a freight broker, then you would set up your clients as a class. You would want to know how much each of your clients paid you. In the end, the final accounts statement will let you know how much money you made, how much your expenses were and what your profits margin are.

Invoicing Clients

As a service provider, your clients will be expecting a bill once the service has been satisfactorily delivered. When you invoice your clients, you want to provide them with detailed information about the services provided. For instance, you might charge a client for moving their cargo. Your clients often have a choice of payment methods and will choose one of four methods. These methods include:

- Flat fee payment
- Fee per mile
- Payment by the hundred weight

When invoicing your clients, you will need to spell out the fee payment method. The flat rate method is pretty obvious. You may, for instance, agree to deliver a package for a client to a particular destination at a fixed price.

Sometimes these are not the only charges to the client. Using accounting software such as QuickBooks will help you process all your income and payments and show you what your profits are, what taxes you need to pay and so on. However, you will need to set it up appropriately before you can begin using it productively.

Bookkeeping and Accounting

Many freight brokers know that they will be involved in some form of accounting and bookkeeping at some point in their business. One of the best places to begin is with the chart of accounts. This chart is essentially a listing of the entire accounting transactions that you might expect to encounter as a freight broker. The list can include some or all of the following:

- Your assets, such as accounts receivable and cash in the bank;

- Liabilities, such as accounts payable and also both income and expenditure are included;

- Income and expenditure, including payments to your shippers and your profits; and

- Expenses, such as loading board fees, office overheads, and telephone costs.

You should assign a certain code or number to each transaction so that it is easy to plug in the figures when doing your accounts. When these figures are entered into your accounting software, you will then receive a financial statement that will let you know about your firm's financial affairs.

The job outlook for a freight broker is promising since it is the fastest growing occupational category within the transportation industry; 29% compared to other occupations. As the economy improves and online shopping increases in popularity, freight brokers are becoming more in demand than ever before. If you still aren't sure about becoming a freight broker then consider the following reasons why you should become a freight broker.

An Independent Career

If you become a freight broker, you are choosing to become your own boss and call all the shots. You can easily start as a single person and then add employees as your grow. Either way, you don't have to worry about working for a boss anymore, and you can make your own decisions.

More Time for Important Things

Being a truck driver means being on the road six days a week or more. Working an office job means being stuck in the 9 to 5, five days a week. All of this takes you away from more important things such as spending time with family and friends or even just taking some time for yourself.

When you're a freight broker, you can set your own work hours, so you'll have more time to spend with family or just relax and do what you want to do. With the smartphones of today, the work of a freight broker has become much easier; you can take your job with you in most cases and enjoy the freedom.

Better Income

As a freight broker you know the industry and you have an industry network worth a lot of money at your disposal. Take advantage of this network access to add additional services to your freight brokerage such as trucking operations, and you'll not only be growing your business but also increasing your income since you won't have others cutting into your revenues.

No Commute

Perhaps the biggest draw for most is the idea of earning a living while working from the comforts of your own home. You can enjoy your lunch and set your own hours. You don't have to get up early only to be stuck in traffic for hours. Plus you have the option to sleep in on occasions. Also, there's no dress code, sounds fun right? Well, it can be.

Low Start-Up Costs

If you have good credit, then you can often start a freight broker career on less than $5,000. This is because you have the flexibility to start from nothing and add on to your workspace and coverage as you want. Read on, and you will see how.

Low Overhead Expenses

If you're working by yourself from home, then you'll be saving a lot of money on overhead costs. Most of your time is spent negotiating on the phone with shippers and carriers or on the computer researching and tracking shipments. This all means a freight broker can keep their expenses as low as $400-$500 per month.

Unlimited Earning Potential

The freight industry is booming, and the only limit to your income is how committed you are to success. As e-commerce grows and flourishes, there is plenty of business to be had for new freight brokers. There are plenty of opportunities for you to earn a lot of money.

Growing Business

The more you grow your freight brokerage business, the more you are increasing your position in the industry. This means you are always building new contacts. This leads to a job that has a never ending expansion potential.

A Family Business

If you have a family, then a freight brokerage can be an excellent way to not only provide for the family but also allow the whole family to get involved. You can start teaching your children about the job and pass it along to them. The possibilities for work your family can do are endless.

A Family Legacy

When you run your freight brokerage right, you can have an asset that takes care of your family for generations to come.

It is clear that there are many benefits to being a freight broker. So now that you're probably on the side of getting into this field, let's consider a little more about the industry to get you the knowledge you need to get started.

Chapter 6: How to find your first Fright broking customers

New trucking businesses rely on load boards alone to find cargos but relying on load boards for business can be extremely limiting. First off, the competition is stiff, and carriers engage in bid wars until profits margins are nearly shaved off. This model of finding work is not sustainable in the long run. If you are serious about growing your trucking company, you must cultivate relationships with your clients, so that you may have repeat business.

Here are some marketing tips that will help you acquire more business for your company.

Social Media

Did you know that you can find potential clients on social media? Yes, your clients are normal people who do normal things but have a need of having their cargo shipped. Starting off, you want to brand your social media pages, whether it is on LinkedIn, Facebook, or Twitter, so that your image may stand out.

Next up, make an effort of joining groups on Facebook that are tailored for truckers, and you will find a lot of information on clients. Other truckers share opportunities with their fellow members.

One key thing to remember while creating your social media pages is to practice honesty. Put the correct information about your services. Also, do not create an account and dump it; you must regularly update your social media pages.

Make a point of marketing your social media to your existing clients and asking them to rate your company. A company that boasts high ratings will attract more attention from potential clients. Having an active social media presence is not only a good marketing method but also a great communication channel for your business.

Follow up On Your Customers

When you finalize business with a client, neither of you is under the obligation to try any harder. But smart business people should try to get their clients' contacts for the purpose of following up on them. Considering that they procured your services, there is a possibility that they will need the same services in the future, and so, if you can create a relationship with them, the client will always contact you whenever they have cargo to be transported. Also, your client can market your business on your behalf by referring their associates to you.

Offer Incentives

Customers love to feel appreciated. When you reward your loyal customers with some incentives, it is a way of showing them that you appreciate their support. Your loyal customers have played a big role in building your business. Also, you should reward customers who refer their friends to your business. You may offer your customers a referral program where if they refer a customer, they get to enjoy a discount or monetary compensation. Communication companies are notorious for using incentives as a way of growing their revenue.

Know Where Your Customers Are Located

It is prudent to first locate where your customers are located so that you may develop a marketing approach. If you fail to identify your customers, you hamper the potential of your business. First, you should try to bring your business as closest as possible to your target customers. Second, you should always ensure that your marketing campaigns are well-targeted. A low-budget marketing campaign that is well-targeted is much more fruitful than a high-budget marketing campaign that is poorly targeted. To grow your company, always go where your customers are.

Create A Website

We are living in an age where people query the Internet for just about anything that they want. And so, if you make an effort of establishing an online presence, you position yourself to attract online customers. All the important details of your company should be available on your site. Moreover, your site should be very well-constructed to make for easy navigation. Also, you should invest in brilliant SEO services so that your website ranks on page one of search engines, for a number of keywords. Thankfully, you can build a website on your own thanks to platforms such as Wix and Weebly that have drag and drop features instead of coding.

Join Trade Associations

Trade associations provide education and networking opportunities to their members. When you join a trade organization for truckers, you get a chance to mingle with other business owners; thus, you are enlightened on more ways of increasing revenue. Never underestimate the potential that you have when you work as a team.

Try To Outdo Your Competitors

One of the best ways to have the upper hand is by outdoing your competitors. Figure out the weaknesses of your competitors and capitalize on them. Customers will flock to your company once you make it seem they are being short-changed elsewhere.

List Your Business On Online Directories

Nowadays, there are online directories, both free and paid, where you may advertise your business. Once you list your company on local and international directories like Yellow Pages, you can expect to have more customers.

Become a Sponsor

It may seem like a costly affair, but the rewards justify the expense. You may sponsor a community event or relevant TV programs, and then you may take that opportunity to create advertising campaigns which boosts brand awareness and sales.

Chapter 7: Tips to running a Successful Freight Brokerage

What are the things that distinguish an average freight broker who manages to break even from a successful freight broker? Here's all the actionable wisdom you need to know about being an ace freight broker.

1. Keep a varied and broad client base.

Keeping a diverse and broad client base is critical to being a successful freight broker. Losing out on one company or customer doesn't seem as heartbreaking if you have a ready database of several other clients to tap into. Top freight brokers understand the value of using a broader customer base so you don't depend on a single company for business. If one company who controls a huge chunk of your revenue moves their business somewhere else, you'll be in trouble. Therefore, even though you may have a few big customers bringing regular business, do not underestimate the power of building a broad client list.

2. Innovate

Another secret for acing the freight broker game is to be open to innovation and newer/more efficient ways of doing things. You can tap into other transportation related enterprises to avoid stagnation. I know freight brokers who have diversified into consulting other freight start-ups, purchasing trucks and becoming carriers. There's plenty of scope for diversification as a freight broker. You can be a one-stop shop for all logistics services. Many trucking company entrepreneurs start off as freight brokers. Keep innovating, adding new services to your business profile and expand your market to grow the business. Learn the ropes of the logistics and transportation business as a freight broker and then transition into building a transportation company.

3. Get rid of defunct carriers

Each trucking company has occasional service issues. However, if there are frequent lapses, you may have to take a call and drop the company from your database. If you are forever having issues with carriers, your clients will quickly move on to another freight broker or trucking company. Of course, initially you can't tell if a carrier is good or problematic. However, over a period of time you'll know the difference between trucks that offer good and snag-ridden service. While you can overlook a one-off case of transportation snag, set some boundaries before it starts affecting your business on a wider scale. Remember, it is not the trucking company but your reputation as a broker that is at stake here. If you enlist too many defunct and problematic companies in your database, it'll put your credibility as a freight broker at stake.

4. Preserve your reputation

The freight broker business is all about networking and building relationships/connections. Focus on building an enviable reputation within the industry if you want to go a long way. Don't take shortcuts or the easy way out if, it's even remotely shady. Have the integrity to pass it even if appears to be a huge opportunity. These things are noticed by people. Plenty of people need reputed, dependable and honest services. If you are able to offer it by keeping your vision firmly fixated on long-term goals, you'll increase your chances of acing the freight broker game.

Build your business on trust and integrity. Word can travel at the speed of a supersonic jet within the industry. Good or bad – companies will know what you are up to and make their business decisions based on your market reputation. One bad experience or one bad practice leading to court loss can damage your business. There will be tough times, and tough decisions to be made but if you want to sustain for long in the freight brokering industry, keep your integrity intact. Do it the right way. Avoid taking shortcuts or looking at quick gains and also focus on maintaining the highest service standards. This way you will increase your chances of having clients who are happy pay for good carrier services and want to associate with frequently.

5. Identify your niche

It is wonderful that you've started a freight broker enterprise. However, what niche are you going to specialize in? This is a good way to be a large fish in a small pond rather than a small fish in a large pond where there are several other fishes waiting for their share of profits. Find a clear niche such as dry van or frozen freight. Trucks and shippers operating in this niche will identify with your services, and you may end up getting a large chunk of profits in these niches. Specialized services will make your brand more sought after. If you are keeping your loads general, segment them effectively through various sections on your website or search function.

6. Join a professional association

Being an active part of any industry needs connections. Join the Transportation Intermediaries Association, which is a trade organization created for third-party logistics service providers. You'll have plenty of professional contacts and networking opportunities. You'll also have access to education matter, top industry trends and codes on the best practices to be followed within the industry. Becoming a part of a professional association has multiple benefits. You'll get to know a lot of people from the industry and get business through referrals and word of mouth.

7. Never Stop Learning

Access to education is no longer a challenge, thanks to the internet. You can access online courses, free webinars, industry cases studies, podcasts, YouTube videos and virtually inexhaustible resources of information for upgrading your knowledge and skills within the freight brokering industry. These resources can help you stay within the industry loop at a marginal cost.

8. Keep in mind the 80-20 rule.

Keep in mind that there are plenty of administrative duties involved in the business of freight brokering. This can be everything from making invoices to maintain a company roster to drafting mails. However, as an agent, you'll need to stay focused only on income generating activities rather than spending a huge chunk of your time in administrative tasks.

Use the 80/20 Pareto Principle, which states that 80 percent of our results come from 20 percent of the input. This means only 20 percent of your activities are accounting for 80 percent of your total results. Use this principle to focus on those tasks that are producing those 80 percent results. Use this rule to also identify those 20% companies or clients that are contributing towards 80% of your output. It is common for 80% percent of a freight broker business' sales to originate from 20% of clients.

How can you use the 80-20 rule to maximize your profits?

First identify the activities that are leading to 80 percent of your sales and then invest more time in those activities. What are your main income producing activities? What are activities that boost your sales? In other words, you are identifying and channelizing those 80 percent activities that are driving more revenue to your enterprise. Maybe, seeking referrals, cold calling, attending networking events, visiting companies is what is doing the trick for you. Once you identify these 20 percent activities, spend more time doing them. This is one of the key secret approaches to growing your freight broker business.

Similarly, use this rule for customers. Identify your top 20 percent clients. These will generally account for about 80 percent of your company's sales. Direct a major share of your sales, promotional and marketing efforts on similar customers. Truth is, not all business activities and customers contribute equally towards the sales generated by your company. Some tasks are harder, others simpler. Some are more time consuming than others. Some have higher value than others. Learn to identify tasks that produce maximum value, and increase them. The idea should be to get good returns on your investment, including time and other resources.

9. Avoid rewriting the rules or reinventing the wheel

While it is good to innovate and diversify, if there's a system already in place don't reinvent the wheel. If you see a majority of successful freight brokers applying a using a specific strategy, service or marketing technique that seems to be working well, incorporate it into your business operations. You don't have to be unique and original all the time. Getting ideas that work from competitors, other freight brokers, logistics companies and truck carriers can lead your business in the right direction. Do what's working for others, and scaling it up with your own business sense.

At times, freight operators look to develop a brand new software system only to learn that there was already a system in place that catered to their needs. Don't waste time doing something different when people are getting results following an existing system.

10. Tone down the sales mode

I'll let you in on a little secret here that goes a long way in helping you gain a loyal customer base for your freight brokering business. Don't talk as if you are selling something. Tone down your sales pitch and speak in a more conversational manner, as if you are talking to family members and friends. Don't launch into sales mode as soon as you see your prospects.

Contrived/manipulated speech patterns, loud, exaggerated tones, slow and hypnotic sales inductions can get on the prospective client's nerves. Speak naturally and appropriately. Make it more conversational and relaxed so the prospect doesn't feel the pressure of doing business with you, which will end up making the prospect of associating with you less desirable. No one wants to talk to a robot who just wants to sell. People like a show of humanity and compassion.

Also, always stay in touch with your contacts. I can't emphasize on this point enough. Sometimes, freight brokers will simply stop communicating with companies or client's that refused their initial business proposal. Yes, they may have opted for another service over yours at the time. However, what's to say that they won't need your services in future. For all you know, they may be having problems with their current service provider or may need additional carriers. Staying in contact with potential customers ensures that yours is the first name that flashes in their mind when they need last minute or emergency bookings. As a freight broker, you'll get plenty of last minute businesses when shippers need carriers urgently. To bag these last minute deals, you have to make an effort to stay on top of the mind of your potential customers even if they have refused business deals in the past.

Send out festival greetings, keep checking periodically, send them messages about new services of features you've added to the business and offer a promo code or discount on the first shipment. Ensure you are the first name that comes to mind for last minute freight transportation deals.

11. Negotiations over the phone

Remember, as a freight broker, you'll have to negotiate plenty of last-minute deals over the phone, which is very different from face to face negotiations. Don't let a customer catch you off guard. Prepare well in advance for the negotiations by clearly knowing your terms. What are the typical statements you will sue to handle objections? What will you say to persuade your clients to agree to your terms? To what extent will you negotiate? Carriers may pose questions about the freight shippers or your customers are wish to move, for which you must have answers ready.

Keep your voice polite, professional and authoritative. Stammering or stumbling for words or appearing flummoxed at the client's questions doesn't help seal the negotiations in your favor.

Also, one of the most important things to keep in mind is while negotiating freight transportations deals over the phone is to stay alert. Do not try to multitask while you are speaking with a driver, shipper, traffic manager, dispatcher etc. Even something as simple as checking a mail can take your focus away from what the person is saying, which could result in a miscommunication, related to shipping terms that the other party may be requesting. Remove the risk of this pointless distraction and focus only on what the person is saying. Your calls and emails can wait until.

12. Take responsibility

Now, now yes you a freight middleman but that doesn't mean you go on telling customers that you are just posting their shipment, nothing else. Though it should be a given this unprofessional and unimpressive at so many levels, freight brokers still do it. What you are doing is telling the shipper that you don't have trucks for their consignment. You have to keep your posture like you are the trucking company that is responsible for transporting their shipment safely and promptly, and not just a middleman whose job ends after dumping the load in a truck. This approach won't help you get many repeat customers.

13. Be unfazed by the bigger firms

There are plenty of mergers, takeovers and acquisitions happening in the freight brokerage industry. This means small business and start-ups may start thinking about their chances among the big fish. How am I going to compete with these giants? Can my business survive after the latest acquisition that happened in town? You are a bee among the elephants. Moving, reacting and maneuvering become faster for you than large organizations with endless policies, codes and hierarchies. Make this work for you! You need a handful of good clients to do good business and spread a good work about your enterprise. The secret is to look at little known sources that the bigger companies won't change touch.

Chapter 8: Licensing and Business Registration

Now that you have gained necessary education and industry experience, you need to move to the next level. The crucial initial steps of setting up your business will involve getting licensed and getting your business registered. To accomplish these tasks, you will need to fill out some paperwork. The process will include:

- Registering your business with the state government
- Applying for a license with the federal government
- Taking out an essential surety bond that covers against unseen hazards

Fortunately, all these processes can be done and completed online. If you have a credit card, a connected computer, and resources to get a hold of all other required forms and fees, then you will be able to accomplish these crucial yet straightforward steps within a few minutes.

Federal Licensing Requirements

Any brokers that ship merchandise across state lines need to seek authorization from the federal government. The arm of the federal government that is responsible for registering freight brokers is the Federal Motor Carrier Safety Administration (FMCSA). When you submit your application forms as well as a small processing fee, you should receive your license within four-six weeks.

Before the year 2015, brokers had to fill out a number of forms and then submit them to the FMCSA either via post or email. However, things have changed since then. What you need to do is make use of the Unified Registration System (URS). The URS puts together all the forms that you need to sign to streamline the application process.

1. Apply for the Operating Authority

One of the initial steps of seeking federal licensing is the application for the operating authority. This is also referred to as the MC number and simply the authority granted to you by the federal government to work as a freight broker. The federal government has an elaborate Unified Carrier Registration process for freight brokers with agents across different cities or towns. You will need to designate an agent or representative within each state where you operate. The federal government normally issues two types of operating authorities:

- Authority for household goods brokers
- Authority for property brokers

To be on the safe side, you should apply for both types of operating authorities, and the good news is, you are actually allowed to do so. Each costs approximately $300. During the license application process, the federal government will request certain information such as:

- Personal and contact information
- Social security number
- Employer identification number

Sometimes the government requires you to obtain a USDOT number if you intend to act as a motor carrier. Therefore, it's best to be ready for this step during the licensing process.

2. Receive a Grant Letter and MC/FF Number

As soon as your application is received and processed, you will receive a MC/FF number. This number is also known as your operating authority granted by the federal government. You will need this number most of the time as you execute your duties. However, even at this stage, you won't have completed the entire process just yet.

First, the federal government, through the Department of Transport, will send you a grant letter. You will have to wait ten days, during which anyone could question your application. After that, you can begin the process of applying for surety bonds. Freight brokers often apply for the BMC-84 bond which is suitable for freight brokers. This is a type of financial protection that is worth $75,000. As a broker, this guarantees your clients compensation – should you fail to adhere to all laws and federal regulations governing the handling and transportation of cargo. Your clients will be free to file a claim for compensation if your actions cause loss or damages.

As a freight broker, you will obtain bonds through agencies such as Lance Surety Bonds. They often collaborate with bond companies that issue the bonds and then back them with financial muscle. During the bond application process, the bond agency will offer you a quote which refers to the cost at which your bond can be obtained. Certain factors will determine this cost. These include certain financial indicators such as your personal credit score. The normal rates range from 1-5% of the total bond amount, usually $75,000.

Once your bond application is approved, the bond company then informs the FMCSA. You will also have the option of entering into a Trust Fund Agreement instead of the surety bond. However, you will have to contribute the full amount of $75,000 to the fund. Most new brokers find this to be a huge challenge, and it tends to lock up financial resources that could be utilized in other ways.

When searching for a suitable bond agency to get a bond, make sure that the chosen agency is affiliated with T-listed and A-rated companies. Such companies are considered financially stable, reliable, and will guarantee to stand by you in case one of your clients files a claim.

3. Apply for Freight Broker Insurance Cover

The freight broker insurance cover is not a mandatory obligation required by law, especially if you intend to operate only as a broker. It is only a requirement for operators who wish to acquire forwarding or carrier authority.

However, while insurance is not a requirement for freight brokers, it is highly recommended. This is because in the course of executing your duties, something may get damaged or lost and you may be held personally responsible. In such cases, the insurance will come in handy. The types of insurance often taken out by truck brokers include liability insurance, property insurance, and cargo insurance. It is especially important to have coverage since some carriers may not purchase insurance for the cargo they are transporting.

Also, when you eventually employ at least two workers, then you will need to acquire workers' compensation insurance. This type of cover is necessary and mandatory for all employers in all states. This is regardless of the type of business that is being undertaken.

Ensure that you confirm with your carriers if they have appropriate insurance cover. There are a number of cases where freight brokers have been sued or pursued for workers' compensation, and successfully so, by employees of carrier companies even when these employees did not work for the brokers. Unless state regulations exempt them from workers' compensation cover, they should have appropriate cover for their workers.

4. Ensure that you Designate Process Agents

As soon as you obtain your FF/MC number, you should then designate your process agents. Your agents need to be designated for each state that you plan to open an office or at least where you intend to have contracts. You are allowed to be an agent within your own state where you have your office and are based. If no one protests your application within the designated protest period, and you were able to comply with all the federal government's requirements, then the FMCSA will proceed to issue you with your freight broker license which will be your operating authority.

If at this point, you have managed to officially become a licensed freight broker, congratulations!

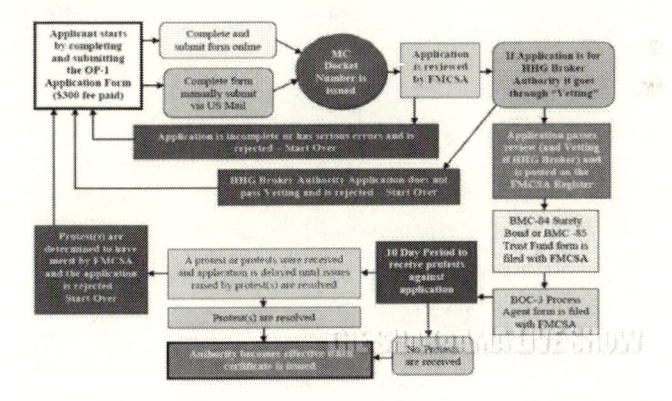

Financial Implications of Becoming a Freight Broker

Are there any huge costs associated with becoming a broker? Inevitably, there are and always will. Here are some costs you need to watch out for:

- Insurance policies
- Operating authority
- Business registration
- Freight broker bond
- Broker training
- Business location and equipment
- Manpower and miscellaneous expenses

These kinds of costs are likely to vary depending on different factors. However, we have taken the time to put a number beside these words:

1. Business Registration

Business registration prices vary in each state. However, according to the Small Business Administration, you can expect to pay roughly between $150-$300 to have your business registered.

2. Operating Authority or License

Expect to pay about $300 for each authority that you wish to change or acquire. For instance, if you wish to get a license as a freight broker and a freight forwarder, then you will pay $300 for each license.

3. Freight Broker Bond Costs

Please note that you will also be required to make some payments for your bond. As it is, the cost of the bond varies and is determined on an individual basis. There are annual premiums to be paid, and these are based on the following factors:

- Experience in the industry
- Financial muscle
- Your credit score

Freight brokers with sufficient experience and excellent credit can expect to pay an annual $900-$3,750 per year. Those with little or no experience and poor credit scores can expect to pay much higher rates, possibly going up to $7,500.

It is advisable to note that the priced offered by different bond companies regularly fluctuates due to competition, losses and changing market conditions. If you want to obtain the best rates in the market, then you should consider signing up with an agency that represents a number of surety bond firms. Such firms can make a comparison of rates across different bond companies and then advise you on the best rates in the market.

Firms such as Lance Surety can provide you with a long list of bond rates as it represents multiple firms. This bond agency has strong relationships with a number of top bond companies that write Freight Broker Bonds. You will be able to obtain very competitive rates if you work with such an agency.

It is important to understand that even those with a poor credit rating can still receive bond. While the rate may not be the same as of those with good ratings, you will still have access to a bond and can proceed with your freight brokerage business. Do not hold yourself back just because you did not get a break.

Cost of Claims

There are other costs that you need to consider besides bond premiums. Your bond's true cost does not just consist of the premiums that you pay annually. It also includes the total amount of liability that could result from any claims filed against you. Should any claims be paid out concerning your bond, then you will most likely be liable to repay the bond company. In most extreme cases, the amounts can be as high as $75,000 plus any associated legal fees.

This is the reason why it is crucial for freight brokers to partner with reliable and trustworthy bond agencies that will treat you with respect and act in your best interest should a claim be made. A reputable bond company will support you all through the bond process including helping to deal with any claims that are filed.

Insurance Policies

Insurance cover is necessary but not mandatory. If you choose to get cover such as contingent cargo insurance, then you can expect annual costs that range from $1,200 to around $1,600. Another type of insurance that you are likely to require is workers' compensation. If you decide to opt for general liability insurance instead, then your insurance costs may rise to about $3,000 annually.

Insurance and other costs are difficult to predict as they will largely depend on your plans for your brokerage firm. However, you can save costs if you adopt some cost-saving measures. For instance, you can work from a home office instead of leasing commercial office space.

And when you start your home office, ensure that you use the home telephone and computer for your work in order to cut back costs. However, you really should invest in good quality broker software that will enable you to operate professionally. A good transport management system can cost approximately $600-$1,200 per annum. Even then, it is bound to be earning a pretty decent income, so it is worth the investment.

Registering and Starting your Freight Brokerage Business

Now that you have all the necessary instruments to operate a freight brokerage business, the next step is to register your business with the state authorities. You will need to form your own Limited Liability Company or LLC. You need to understand how the process goes so that you can do it yourself with ease. If you find the process too challenging or complex, then you can hire a lawyer for some advice. preferably the ones who specializes at drafting and setting up businesses. However, we think that the process is pretty simple and straightforward. See the steps below:

1. Identify a suitable business name that conforms to the state's business registration rules.
2. Prepare your paperwork by filling out all the necessary forms and providing all the required information, including personal details and contact information.

3. Once the paperwork is ready, submit it all together with all required attachments. Accompany the paperwork with the required fees. The fees can range anywhere from $100-$800 depending on the rules and your state.

4. Now come up with a suitable LLC operating agreement which role is to indicate the rights and responsibilities of LLC members. Once these are published, you then need to publish a notice of intent that lets the general public known that you wish to form an LLC. Follow this procedure only if it is a requirement in your state.

5. Once your business is registered, you can then proceed to apply for other licenses and permits necessary for operations.

The Business Registration Process

The process of registering your business begins at the office of the Secretary of State within your state. The registration procedures will vary from state to state. However, the process generally begins with your secretary of state's office.

Sometimes you may be required to head over to the local tax office, at the Department of Revenue, to register as a taxpayer. Business tax registration is crucial if you are to operate legally, as required. When registering your business, you will not be limited only to a Limited Liability Company. There are other options available as well. They include the following:

- Partnership
- Sole proprietorship
- Corporation
- Limited liability company

As you choose the best fit for your business, remember that there is no wrong or right choice. What matters is identifying the most suitable form of business that you require.

Learn About Truck Load Boards

A load board or freight board is a matching system online that lets freight brokers and shippers post loads. The boards also provide for transporters or carriers to post any free equipment in their possession. This makes it easy for carriers and shippers to find each other and then draft agreements that enable them to work together to move cargo.

Many of these load boards are sophisticated platforms. They allow users, shippers, brokers, and transporters, to search or post loads using a particular criterion. The load boards also provide additional services to carriers and freight brokers. Some of these additional services include the following:

- Message boards,
- FMCSA verification
- Load Matching
- Financing of pre-approved loads
- Capacity to note info on shippers and carriers
- Mobile access
- The necessary credit information

You can find a number of load or freight boards out there. Some are free while others charge a fee. The paid ones can be quite costly. You can expect to pay about $100 per month to gain access. Keep in mind that you get exactly what you pay for.

Just remember that paid load boards are not always the best so you should keep searching until you find the one that is perfect for your business.

While load boards are useful, they do have their pros and cons. For instance, if you are a new operator, you are likely to find lots of great opportunities on the board. However, the problem is that they have too many players and this tends to reduce margins and increase competition to unhealthy levels.

Factoring Invoices through the Load Board

Many load boards integrate loads together with firms that provide freight bill factoring. The integration enables freight brokers to take on slow-paying freights so it is a useful feature when you are running low on funds. You get access to crucial financing that can help you pay for any repairs, fuel, and the driver. You can also use the funds to take additional loads to expand your operations.

As a truck broker, you will often find that freight bills take pretty long to get settled. Sometimes even more than sixty days. In such instances, you may require finances to meet your regular or recurrent expenditure. This is where bill factoring comes in handy. It allows you to gain access to much-needed funds which you can use as you see fit. You can easily factor invoices through a load board. Here is how it is done:

Freight Bill Factoring Process
- Deliver a consignment to your client
- Then send an invoice to the client and a copy to the funder
- Once these are received, the advanced funds will be wired to you
- The transaction will then be completed once your client pays

What are the Benefits of Bill Factoring?
- You enjoy predictable funds access
- Approvals are often quite fast
- You have access to pay drivers, repairs, and fuels
- Sometimes it comes with fuel cards

Always ensure that you choose the correct factoring company to partner with. You should also find out how long it will take them to send you funds to finance your initial freight bill. All these are crucial when seeking a funding firm to engage with.

Negotiate the Best Terms

You should be able to engage the company and enter into negotiations to receive the very best terms. The profit margins in the transport sector are minimal, so it is difficult to find wiggle room. The margins are tight mainly due to stiff competition in the industry. Therefore, the costs will depend on:

- Your shippers and agents' credit
- Extra or additional fees
- Factoring rate
- Factoring advance

Once your business is up and running, you should ensure that you acquire the correct software. Good quality software can make a huge difference to your business. For instance, quality Transport Management Software (TMS) can help you manage your records and paperwork, plan routes appropriately, dispatch drivers, send invoices, and even set up shipping well in advance. Should a crisis arise, then you can use the tools provided to sort out the crisis.

You will be required to be online most of the time. Truck or freight brokering is as much about computers and the Internet as it is about consignments and deliveries. Online platforms such as the modern ones that you will be using are competing seriously with the traditional phone and fax machines. There are apps in the market today that you can use to help manage your business and increase efficiency. Unfortunately, some apps in the market are trying to eliminate brokers from the equation and trying to link consigners or shippers with transporters. Try and find shippers who use standardized shipments that require standard trucks. Sometimes you will need to get into direct contact with firms that provide specialized shipping.

Setting Up your Freight Brokerage Business

Now that you have completed most of the essential processes, you are more than ready to begin work. One of the most crucial steps you need to follow is to establish credibility. As a newcomer, no truck company or client will touch you with a ten-foot pole unless you can prove that you have the necessary authority as well as surety bonds. It is only after you are properly registered, licensed, and possess all the essential authority to operate as a freight broker that you begin getting clients and loads.

You will also need to get your finances in order. Many truckers are wary of freight brokers who dish out jobs but do not have the finances to pay for the service.

It is also important, if you feel the need, to start off as an agent. An agent is basically one who works for an established broker. You can be in a different location with your own office, but the experience is invaluable. Once you receive sufficient experience as an agent, you can then set up yourself as a freight broker. This also provides an excellent way of acquiring your own clients.

It is advisable to expect to hurt and lose money in the first year of business. Unless you are really good or have sufficient experience, a lot of new freight brokers barely break even in the first year. However, if you hang in there, you should start enjoying success. You should expect to foot your costs and expenses for a while so be prepared for that.

Legal Process Agents

Once your business picks up and you want to set up offices in another state, then you should get an agent. You will need an agent in each state to represent you there. Officially, they are referred to as legal process agents. You are required by law to register the legal process agents in each state where they operate. Agents are often registered with the federal government transport department through the FMCSA. You will need to fill out and submit form number BOC-3. You will be charged a processing fee of about $50 with each BOC-3 form that you submit.

Chapter 9: Obtaining Freight: Brokers vs. Direct Shippers

At the end of the day, the main thing is that you must find loads to carry. As a new business operator, you will find yourself relying on load boards for work which is usually not a sustainable model. However, if you can get in the good books of regular freight brokers or regular shippers, then you can be assured of enough jobs that will even push you to expand your business.

To ensure that your trucking company stays in business, you must be willing to pursue only the methods that have been proven successful. The secret of being a successful owner-operator lies in your ability to grow your list of shippers who can trust your services.

Make Technology Your Friend

Understand that when you reach out to a direct shipper without the help of a broker, you stand to gain more. Through platforms such as DAT, PC Miller, and Truckstop, you may be able to contact shippers and make a deal. Also, you should get into Internet marketing. This is where you advertise your services on websites where your sure shippers hang out and get their contact details through your sales funnel so you may contact them again through email to sell your services. The two most powerful forms of online marketing are banners and native advertising.

Cold Call

Some carriers focus only on the administrative aspects of the work, perhaps under the illusion that if they deliver great services, clients will come. Well, that is a correct assumption, but the trouble is that the trucking industry is terribly competitive. It is hard to get constant loads from a shipper without investing in that relationship. You have to be aggressive about it and ask around for contacts of shippers and call them. The rate of rejection is high, but you should not be distracted by the rejection as you will eventually find someone who will give you a chance.

Have An Online Presence

When you contact brokers, but they do not want to work with you, it usually is a problem about your overall image. Serious brokers want to work with authorized and high-quality carriers. If a broker referred a shipper to a carrier who turned out to be mediocre, the shipper may blame the broker, and possibly ditch their services. Brokers also do not have the time to spend the whole day chatting you up. They just go to your website where you have uploaded all the important information, and they will reach a decision quickly.

Ask Around Your Contacts

Shippers are just ordinary people who need their cargo to be moved. You might be surprised that there are many shippers in your circles; all you have to do is actively seek them out. Start by approaching owners of companies that you are affiliated with. And then introduce your services to them and give them a fair rate. If they have been looking for a carrier, or if you have given them a better deal than what they had elsewhere, that is all the more good. Most successful carriers know how to start and maintain relationships with shippers.

Chapter 10: How to Get the Best Drivers

Having the best drivers might make the difference between the success and failure of your company. A great driver will be careful not only in delivering loads but also in expenditure. A great driver should have a sense of economy; keeping in mind that the profit margins are small especially at the beginning.

However, it can be quite challenging to find a driver who fits the bill. The trucking industry is plagued by the constant movement of drivers as they seek greener pastures. This shows that a lot of drivers are not satisfied with their work environment. Regardless of these challenges, you can still fish out a great driver when you take the appropriate measures.

Here are some of the ways to ensure that you find hardworking and loyal drivers.

Pay Well

When you pay your drivers well, they are motivated to do their part extremely well. Also, they will be less tempted to commit fraud. On the whole, the industry rates are quite low. Those who can afford to pay extremely well seem to be the long-established fleets that enjoy a high income. Unless the freight rates go up, some owners cannot afford to give their drivers a decent salary.

A great method to work around this problem is to offer a flat rate and a performance based on remuneration. This will make the driver want to work a little bit harder so that they may secure large commissions.

Involve The Drivers

Take the time to find out the views of drivers. Sometimes working for a big company might make a driver feel like a cog in a wheel, and if anything bothered them, they would not bring it up. When you set up systems through which drivers can communicate, you show them that you value their contribution. Also, you should be a bit more intentional when devising new plans for your business. For instance, if you plan to start operations on a new route, you may want to ask about their views. When you show a driver that they are a part of the business, they will be less inclined to flee when the opportunity occurs.

Ask For Referrals

Perhaps this is the best method of hiring. Your fellow business owners are well aware of a number of drivers. And so, if you have an open position, you should go to them first. This way, you increase your odds of finding an experienced driver.

Colleagues are aware of what certain drivers are like, and they may guide you when you need to fill a position. In the trucking industry, there are a lot of unhinged drivers – some are flippant with work or even criminals. Bad experiences with drivers may translate into losses. Also, take care as to whom you solicit referrals. Not everyone would love to see you working with the best.

Use The Internet

In as much as the referral is the best method of looking for drivers, you must understand that there are capable drivers who lack civilian networks. You may use the Internet to reach such drivers.

There are job boards, Facebook groups, and online communities catered to drivers. And so, you may want to post your requests here and go through the responses. When you hire a driver from the Internet, it is prudent to put them on probation to see what they are really like before accepting them wholly into your business.

Another method of looking for a driver through the Internet is by organizing a contest for drivers.

Be Honest

When you are hungry for a driver, you might be tempted to sugarcoat the reality. This never works. For instance, if you lie about work hours or routes, you might cause the driver to resent you. And when enough resentment builds up, the driver will most likely run off. When you are honest, you set the tone for conducting business. But when you lie, you might tempt your driver to lie also – if only as a way to fit into the apparent company culture. So, recruiters must resist the urge of creating unrealistic expectations in the minds of drivers.

Onboarding

When you have a new hire, you should not just brief them on their tasks and send them on their way. Instead, you should practice the fine art of onboarding. This is where you inform your new hires of the rules, regulations, and procedures so that they may assimilate well into the company. It is a chance to project the image of having a community.

As the manager or owner, you may want to have a sit-down with a new hire over lunch in order to orient them about the business, and afterward, the new hire should meet everyone who is involved in the day-to-day operations of the business.

Having a proper onboarding procedure gives the new hire a sense **of belonging.**

Put Driver Health First

The job itself is hectic, but you may want to show your driver that you care. You should also invest in facilities like gyms, and promote habits such as healthy eating, exercising, and on-site screenings. Having healthy drivers discourages absenteeism, and your business may run without glitches.

Also, your payment packages should be inclusive of sick leaves. For instance, when a driver is sick at home, they should have the security of a salary.

Handle Problems That Drivers Raise

Besides low pay, another factor that forces drivers to quit jobs is the failure by management to attend to their concerns. A great company should put the needs of its drivers first, which means their problems should be resolved as quickly and humanely as possible. When the needs of the drivers are met, they feel respected and more obligated to play their part well. However, when the concerns of the drivers are ignored, it usually causes a buildup of resentment which only results in driver-exodus.

Chapter 11: Determine the Best Area of Operation

The area of operation also influences the success of your business. You must work in an area that is in harmony with your business. Always make sure that your area of operation suits not only your business but also your staff and economic concerns.

Here are some of the critical factors to consider in selecting your area of operation.

Competition

As you know, the trucking industry is extremely competitive, but that should not discourage you from joining the industry, considering that the market is huge. That means about 70% of freight is hauled by trucks! So, despite the competition, there are still opportunities.

It is upon you to study an area where there is the right balance of clients, and the competition is manageable. If you set up your business in an area that is dominated by another trucking company, you will have trouble finding clients. You need to stand out by adding a mix to your services.

Proximity To Other Businesses And Complementary Services

The success of a trucking company depends on the input of other personnel. Your trucks will need various personnel like mechanics, servicemen, casual workers, and managers. And so, you have to make sure that your business is established in an area where complementary services are within easy reach. When you fail to take this into account, you only increase your operation costs which eat into your revenue. Furthermore, you may want to establish your trucking company near another company, so that you have more opportunities in the sense that your business will capitalize on existing customer traffic.

Infrastructure

A trucking company will need rigid structures and facilities for smooth operation. Keeping this in mind, you might want to look for a region with the best infrastructure. You should also evaluate the types of road and ensure that your truck is fit for a specific type of road. When you operate out of an area with great facilities, your trucks will have a much longer shelf life as opposed to operating out of an area with poor infrastructure. Apart from simplifying your operations, being in an area with great infrastructure will open you up to more opportunities.

Expenses

When you bring your expenses down, you may increase your revenue margin. So you should always consider the aspect of cost when determining an area of operation. You want to be in an area where the costs of utilities are favorable, not only for the business but also for the employees. This means high-end residences are out of the question unless they are your target customers. See to it that you are in an area where expenses such as rent, janitorial services, repairs, and amenities are favorable. This will help your company have a bigger profit margin.

Laws

You want to run away from jurisdictions where laws are oppressive. For instance, you might want to set up your trucking business in a state that offers tax breaks as opposed to a state that imposes burdensome rules and regulations in the trucking industry.

No matter where you go, you cannot evade taxes, but you can choose to operate from an area where the tax laws are favorable. Trucking businesses are subject to different tax laws in various states. And so it is upon you to find out the state whose laws are most favorable to your business.

Style of Operation

What is the style of business that you are going to use? There are various methods of presenting your business to the world. Ideally, you want the philosophy of your business to stand out and yet keep the business sides of things. Thus, you have to select an area that is well-aligned with your business values. Having a particular style is critical because it contributes to the overall image of your business. When you set up a trucking company, one of your main selling points is your style. Customers may be drawn to you because of your style of operation, and selecting an appropriate location is necessary.

Demographics

You may want to evaluate the statistical data of people. This will give you a clear picture of your target audience.

First off, you have to mark your potential customers and their proximity to the location of your business. You have to position your business in an area where your customers have easy access.

Also, you have to look at the financial ability of your target market. You should bring your business closer to the people who have the ability to spend, especially those who are gainfully employed or are involved in other commercial activities.

Also, you should see to it that you are in an area where there are enough people to offer you the varied services and skills that your business may need.

Communication

Communication plays an extremely vital role in the trucking business. Think about this. You are in the business of looking for cargo to transport, and thus you will have to keep communicating with freight brokers and shippers in order to get loads. The worst that could happen is a communication barrier because you will not be able to come to an agreement. You should also be aware of the channels that most of your customers love using. You may find that in a certain area, load boards are popular while clients in another area prefer doing things the traditional way – making calls.

Space

Owning a trucking company requires space, especially if you operate a fleet. For this reason, you will find that it can be challenging to establish a trucking company in the middle of a city. It is critical to have a facility where your trucks are parked. And so, when you scout for an area of operation, you have to consider the availability of space. Also, you should consider the type of buildings and future plans. Obviously you intend to expand your business so you might want to be in a geographical place that will not limit you when you are ready to expand.

Chapter 12: Analyze Your Competition

The trucking industry is very competitive. Customers have the luxury of choosing what company they want to work with. In the face of competition, companies have to develop close ties with customers. But regardless of competition, the core qualities of a successful business still do apply. It is vital to see how you stack against other companies. In the trucking industry, aggressive marketing is embraced considering the steep competition. Look for the weaknesses of other companies and capitalize on them.

Price

Gather information about your competitor's pricing plans. Generally, there are industry limits, and you would not find a quote beneath a certain figure. No matter how desperate your company may be, you have to respect the industry by enforcing the limit as it makes no business sense to operate at a loss. However, some of your competitors may be greedy. In such cases, you are at liberty to offer their customers sweeter deals. In this situation, you may engage in direct marketing efforts to their customers and show them how much they would save if they took up your offer.

Quality

When it comes to selecting carriers, customers are spoilt for choice. So you cannot afford to provide poor services. Customers want to work with consistent carriers. In your marketing efforts, you might want to single out carriers whose services are poor and try to attract their customers. Now, what consists of poor services in the trucking industry?

- Failure to beat deadlines
- Lack of necessary paperwork
- Inexperienced and incompetent personnel

- Poor packaging and transportation

You should present your company as a provider of quality services and highlight the areas that your competitors are weak on.

Add-on services

Customers love working with shippers who throw value-adding services into the deal. Actually, it is one of the secrets of retaining your customers. Try to find out whether your competitors offer add-on services, like cargo segmentation and integrations, or just dump the cargo and race off to the next gig. Offering additional services is a clever marketing tactic that gives customers a reason to stick with your company. However, do not stretch yourself too much as additional services may be costly in both monetary and time factors.

Inventory

Sometimes, customers may work with carriers who have limited resources. For instance, if the carrier does not have enough trucks, it may lead to a lot of time wastage, and it is bad for business. You might want to attract customers from other carriers and bring them to you by virtue of having a stable company. This indicates that your company has a sound financial platform and can deliver quality services. In an industry plagued with inferior services, customers give positive reactions to carriers that demonstrate excellence.

Chapter 13: Important Gear and Tools

The driver gets to enjoy an adventurous life. When your job requires you to be on the road, you are definitely going to have a memorable time of it. But you can only have a great time when you are comfortable. Being a driver is no easy task. There are various tools and gear that you will have to bring along so that you may have a great experience while on the road. In as much as you may want to bring along all your necessities, it is advisable to travel as light as you can.

Here are some of the gear and tools that you should bring along:

Emergency Gear

This line of work can be very unpredictable. Having emergency gear is a great protective measure. When emergencies come up, you will not be helpless. Some of the things that make up the emergency gear include weather gear, light reflective clothes, road flares, and chains for reigning tires in when the snow falls.

Toolbox

Trucks experience minor glitches while on the road, and you need a toolbox in order to correct such minor problems. A toolbox comprises the following parts: zip ties, brake-cleaner, pliers, screwdriver, hammer, wrench set, pocket knife, tire pressure gauge, flashlight, and batteries.

Portable Toilet

You need to have a portable toilet so that you are not uncomfortable during the trip. This is crucial for both hygiene and economic sense.

Indoor Sleeping Bag

Of course, you will need to have a place for sleeping. An indoor sleeping bag may not be the most comfortable place to sleep, but it is far better than sleeping on the wheel.

Aluminum Walk Ramp

A walk ramp is useful in transferring the load in and out of the truck. It is especially useful when there is not a loading dock or when the lift on the back of the truck's rig is not working.

Sunglasses

While you are on the road, expect climatic conditions to keep changing across various regions. You want to have sunglasses to shield you against the hot sun. Also, when you are in a dusty area, you might want to put your sunglasses on. Sunglasses are also important for aesthetic purposes.

Gloves

The ideal gloves are made of leather. A great pair of leather gloves is essential, particularly when you are handling goods that pose a health risk. Ensure that you get new gloves every now and then so that the quality may not be compromised.

First aid kit

You are likely to hurt yourself either on a narrow and wide road. This necessitates a first aid kit, and in case of an emergency, you will have a way of administering first aid to yourself or another member of your crew.

Slow cooker

Truck drivers are notorious for having a bad diet. This is understandable considering that they are always in a rush to deliver loads, which denies them time to worry about their health concerns. Thanks to modern technology, drivers can now afford to cook while they drive! And so, you may consider bringing along a slow cooker with you to prepare your food as you drive. This is a very important investment because healthy eating means you won't come down with an illness and thus have to take time off work.

6 Gallon Jugs

During the long hauls, you will obviously need an ample supply of water whether it is for keeping yourself clean, cooling down the engine, or quenching your thirst. The 6 gallon jugs are best suited for storing water as they are made of sturdy material and shaped conveniently.

Mini-fridge

The internal atmosphere of a truck is not the best for storing perishable goods like fruits and vegetables. Having a mini-fridge ensures that you can keep your fruits and vegetables fresh as well as keep drinks cold.

Ratchet and Winch Straps

Straps are most especially useful for tying down heavy loads. Ratchet straps are used for specific weights and are controlled by a hand crank, and winch straps can withstand higher tension and heftier loads.

Space Blanket

The space blanket will heat you up during those cold nights. The blanket is designed for your body heat not to escape, thus keeping you warm. Space blankets are not only warmer than fur blankets, but they are also compact which makes them easier to carry.

A Shower Kit

Do not let your job excuse you from taking a shower. You should have a shower kit that will enable you to take regular showers. You may convey a great image to your business partners, and you can be taken seriously if you are clean.

Laptop

Considering that records are very sensitive in this industry, a laptop is a great computing device for keeping updated and accurate records. Also, you can use the laptop to access management software.

Wi-Fi Gadget

In this age, the Internet has almost become a necessity. The importance of the Internet to a driver on the move cannot be overstated. For one, when you have Internet, you can hardly get lost as you navigate your way through the states. Whenever you have a concern, you may first conduct an Internet search before turning to other means. Also, the Internet is a great entertainment tool. Through the Internet, you can read books, listen to music, and play games.

Boots and Jacket

You are going to be in rough environments most of the time. So, you will need to have a nice pair of boots and a jacket to shield you against the cold.

Vacuum Cleaner

Being on the road for most of the day will expose your truck to dirt. But you must ensure that you observe great hygiene standards. Having a vacuum cleaner is a great option of minimizing the dust and keeping the truck clean.

Air Freshener

The cargo that you transport may not only make the back of your truck dirty but also stink it up. For this reason, you need to have an air freshener to spray after cleaning the back of the truck.

Charger

Considering that you will be away on the road, you have to carry the charger so that important devices like your phone and laptop will not shut down. Nowadays, most trucks are fitted with sophisticated systems that allow you to charge your devices while on the road.

Contact List

The trucking business requires the input of various personnel. You have to work with people to complete your mission. And thus, you have to keep a contact list of the people that are most important to your mission. It is prudent to have your list written in longhand just in case your communication device fails to work.

Chapter 14: How to Scale Your Business

Most registered trucking companies in the US are small companies. Evidently, scaling up is quite the challenge, but make no mistake, it is doable. There are many owners of fleets and a large percentage of these people begun from the bottom. So how did they do it? What are the secrets for scaling up your trucking company?

Seek Financing

You have to seek financing. The thing that underscores the statement "scaling up" is a need for more trucks. You can only have more trucks when you have tons of money. Well, you do not need to have **all** of the money to buy trucks. You can arrange for a loan with a money-lending institution and settle for the payment plan that suits you. Borrowed funds should not only be used to acquire new trucks but also to improve service delivery. The more capital you have, the better services you may give your clients.

However, you must be very careful about how you invest borrowed money because if you drown the funds in unworthy investments, there will be hell to pay. You risk driving your company into bankruptcy and ruining yourself financially.

Find Profitable Loads

When you are new to the business, it can be really challenging to find customers. The terrible deals on load boards will seem quite enticing. However, you should do your maximum best to find profitable loads. You will not find these kinds of cargos on load boards. Profitable loads can only be found through establishing relationships with clients. You may find high-paying clients through freight brokers or your own efforts. When you have the trust of your clients, they bring business to you. This gives you a reason to expand. Move as fast as you can from load boards.

Resolve Issues

The trucking industry is a high-stress zone. Calls may come from every side, delivering depressing news, and making you want to explode. But you must learn the art of resolving issues as quickly as they come instead of letting them pile up and then bursting.

The trucking business involves a lot of paperwork. You must put systems in place to ensure that every process is smooth-sailing. If this is beyond you when you are managing only one truck or a small company, you won't be able to manage a fleet where the processes will be obviously heftier and more challenging. You can discover new methods of improving the efficiency of your office by talking to experienced truckers.

Ensure that you have Steady Cash Flow

There is nothing as stressful to a driver as when they need money, but there is a shortage of it. Such a driver will be on the lookout for a better company. Always ensure that there is a constant supply of cash in the office. This will guarantee faster delivery of services and put you in good standing with your clients. When you have a steady flow of cash, you are able to pay for fuel, drivers, and repairs. You can also take on more jobs.

Have a Plan

Your plan should not just exist in your head; it should be put into writing as a business plan. When you have an original and ambitious business plan, it will make all the difference regardless of what your challenges might be. For instance, the lending institutions will want to extend their loan to you, investors will want to be part of your business, and key personnel will want to work with you too. The challenge is to come up with a great business plan. Of course, when you draft a business plan, you might imagine it is the best ever which might not be the case. Therefore, you should seek the assistance of an expert

Retain Your Drivers

The trucking industry is expanding at a huge rate, but surprisingly the workforce isn't. The American Trucking Association says that the shortage of drivers is fast escalating into a crisis. Thus, retaining drivers can be quite challenging considering that companies with a shortage of drivers are tirelessly wooing your driver for an apparently better deal. This is a major challenge that you must beat. You retain drivers by paying decent salaries, making their working conditions great, and making them feel part of the company, not just a driving robot.

Work with Factoring Companies

Shippers and clients may take forever to pay you, but your business must keep running, so where should you get the money? Working with factoring companies that can buy your accounts receivable gives you up to a 90% advance, and then eventually collects the payment from your customer. Factoring is one of the primary ways that trucking companies resolve their cash flow problems. However, you might want to conduct due diligence before working with a factoring company, just to be sure that they are both experienced and trustworthy.

Make Use of Technology

The trucking industry has benefited a lot from technological advancement. Software that handles most management tasks for trucking companies has been developed, and its users report saving more time and increasing profits. Technology can give you a handle on all your trucks and show you real-time updates. You may integrate the following Apps into your management software to increase functionality:

KeepTruckin

It allows you to track daily driver logs. You can get violation alerts and working hours recap.

Trucker Tools

This App shows you the critical information such as traffic, weigh-scale, and weather conditions.

GasBuddy

It helps you to find gas stations by price or distance parameters.

Chapter 15: What to Expect in the First Two Years

Like any other business, the early stage of operating a trucking business can be challenging. Especially if you are starting out in the industry, you will face challenges from every side. However, once you grow out of these challenges, your business may stabilize and even start to expand.

Driver turnover

The trucking industry faces a high rate of driver turnover. Driving can be extremely tedious considering that you may be away for two weeks straight. This affects most drivers' emotional and mental health, and the situation is worsened by the fact that most drivers do not take home a lot of money. All of these unfavorable conditions make drivers very unstable. They are always on the lookout for the next big opportunity. As a business, when your drivers are moving at a quick rate, it may hamper your ability to deliver. One of the major steps of ensuring that your drivers stick around with you is to offer them good pay and ensure that their schedule allows emotional nourishment. Also, encourage them to raise their opinions about the company and steps to improve service delivery.

Cash flow

One of the biggest challenges that trucking companies (both new and established) struggle with is insufficient funds. This may not necessarily mean that the company is not finding enough loads to ship; instead, many debtors have not paid yet.

If your company faces cash flow problems while you have debtors, you may sell your accounts receivable to factoring companies and acquire immediate funds. Cash flow problems can be extremely limiting because they deter your company from being able to take on more loads or force your company into providing poor services that drive the customers away.

Maintenance Expenses

Trucks are some of the most expensive vehicles to maintain. This is particularly true for trucks that travel over long distances. At the two-year mark, various parts of your trucks will have started to suffer wear and tear, calling for replacements. It is always prudent to cater for repair and maintenance through fuel cards as opposed to cash or credit cards. When you use fuel cards, you will be much more able to track your expenses.

Technology

The trucking industry has received a major boost from technological advancement. After two years, you may be managing a small fleet, and it would be extremely challenging to do it manually. Thankfully, there is technology to ensure that management and all other vital tasks are deployed from one platform. Using trucking management software, you may be able to tell where your trucks are located and provide better customer care services. Using the right technology can reduce your workforce and grow your revenue.

Expansion or closure

Two years of operation are enough to give you an idea of the fate of your company. You will have sufficient evidence whether to continue operations or just abandon your venture. One of the useful tips to survive in this industry is to start small and expand your company as your sales grow. Never get into debt in order to expand your company.

Chapter 16: Secret Tips to Increase Profit of Your Trucking Business

At the end of the day, the most important thing is that your business makes a profit, and it doesn't hurt to extend your profit margins. The habits that will help you increase your profits are pretty much known by everyone. It is the usual stuff: be punctual, handle your paperwork, take care of your customers, and reward your drivers.

However, these are the not-so-known secrets of increasing the profits of your trucking business:

Outsource the dispatch department

The dispatch department ensures that the orders are matched with the appropriate driver. They play a vital role in the trucking industry. However, the dispatchers can be quite expensive in the United States, and their average cost is $1,400 per week. You may work around this by outsourcing your dispatchers to Europe. It is a great cost-reduction measure considering that it would cost $400 per week.

Use fuel cards

A fuel card is an effective way of easing your paperwork, and it eases the process of tracking your expenses. Fuel cards also make much economic sense because they entitle the user to discounts and rebates. The discounts might seem small at first, but eventually, these little amounts add up to quite a substantial amount. Fuel cards also offer critical safety measures, as the driver no longer has to move around with cash which can make him a target. Considering that you can impose limits on the type of transactions you can have with a fuel card, this goes a long way in managing expenses.

Seek freight factoring deals

Freight factoring, also known as trucking factoring, is an arrangement where trucking companies sell their accounts receivable to a factoring company. Considering that payments are made long after carriers have made the delivery, an owner-operator may be in cash straits. And so, the owner-operator may decide to sell their invoice to a factoring company who will eventually get paid by the customer. Upon submitting the invoice, the owner-operator receives an advance on terms that the balance will be cleared later when the customer pays. This is a great method of ensuring the normal operations of your business.

Secure a great deal for your trucking company insurance

For one, the trucking business can be very risky. What would happen if you hired a junkie and they went out and crashed your truck? If you don't have the right insurance cover, it could mean a financial disaster. Go through the policies, be informed, and resist making decisions based on your emotions alone. Having a great insurance coverage will boost client confidence. Considering that regular shippers want to work with carriers who are serious about insurance, it could mean more business for you.

Install GPS on trucks

Installing GPS on your fleet is a major step forward. Thanks to GPS, you can stop calling drivers every now and then just to ask where they are which is painfully annoying. You can always check up on where they are without interrupting them with never-ending calls. Also, you can keep concerned customers updated on the progress of their cargos and help them estimate the time their load arrives. In the unfortunate instance that the truck is stolen, it would be very easy to locate it especially by following the GPS signal. Also, GPS sends automatic alerts when the truck leaves without authorization. Having GPS makes economic sense because it saves you from troubles that would have otherwise cost you a lot.

Install fuel theft prevention systems

You would be surprised to know that fuel theft is more common than people think. It is estimated that an average truck may lose up to $1,000 worth of fuel to thieves every month, and that is a shocking figure! To protect yourself against being set back $1,000 every month, you may want to fit a fuel theft prevention system.

Purchase maintenance plan (Penske, Ryder)

This is a great tactic of reducing maintenance expenses.

Give drivers specialized training

Train and educate drivers on safe driving. Make them drop unhealthy habits like dividing their attention while driving. Great drivers are the biggest investment of a trucking company. They are the force behind a growing trucking company. One of the reasons that contribute to a high turnover of drivers in trucking companies is the loss of respect. When you train your drivers, it is actually a show of respect, and you are more likely to retain them.

Use cloud-based software for management purposes

Powerful trucking management software simplifies things. It can help you handle mind-numbing paperwork. You can use the software to perform accounting tasks, create invoices, and send the invoices to your debtors. Trucking management software helps you to manage fleets; if you approached each truck at a time, it would be incredibly monotonous and tiresome. Management software improves data accuracy, decreases inventory costs, and extends the profit margins.

Chapter 17: Office Personnel: Safety Coordinator, Broker, Salesperson & Dispatcher

A trucking company requires the input of skilled personnel in order to succeed. They are responsible for the administrative, managerial, and clerical duties. When a company has a strong team in the office, the success is sure.

Safety Coordinator

You have to understand that the trucking industry is full of risks, and companies fork out billions in compensating their injured workers. Considering the high risk in the trucking industry, companies opt to hire safety coordinators to make the processes as safe as possible. This is a great investment that saves companies from paying billions to its workers.

Whenever there is an accident in the workplace, the safety coordinator is called to investigate. The goal of an investigation is to find out the cause of the accident, and whether the employees had followed the stipulated safety guidelines. The safety coordinator reports their findings and then works with employees to avoid such accidents in the future. The safety coordinator enforces the plan and monitors the outcome.

Employers should offer safety training to their employees, especially on matters involving fire and hazardous material. A safety coordinator should conduct regular inspections in order to spot potential hazards and nip them. Inspections also help determine whether the drivers are operating within safety guidelines and if they are in need of more safety training. The Occupational Safety and Health Administration encourage employees to come forth about work-related injuries, but the forms have to be approved by the safety coordinator.

Freight Broker

A freight broker is an individual or a company that connects shippers with authorized carriers. Freight brokers play a pivotal role in the trucking industry. They are well-connected with shippers, and as a new business owner, you may want to have good relationships with freight brokers so that they may send business your way.

Freight brokers are very resourceful and play a huge role in facilitating movement of cargos. They earn commissions by helping carriers connect with shippers and strike a deal to transport their loads. A shipper who doesn't have any connections with an authorized carrier contacts a freight broker, who in turn connects them with a reliable carrier.

Brokers can come from any background, but the key to success is being great at establishing relationships with shippers. A freight broker who has won the trust of regular shippers will have more orders than they can handle, but a freight broker who cannot create meaningful relationships with shippers usually ends up frustrated.

A freight broker may have an agent representing them, and the agent's work is similar to what a broker does, but the agent obviously represents the broker's interests. Experienced brokers have liability insurance that covers shipper's cargo in the event when the carrier's insurance fails. Brokers who provide insurance coverage are the best as it is indicative that they have a strong financial foundation and can offer quality services.

Salesperson

Every trucking company aims to hire a competent salesperson because he or she could make or break the company. A great salesperson is successful at selling the company. They provide solutions to clients at great rates.

One of the core duties of a salesperson is to move around the assigned territory and talk to customers in person on a regular basis. A great salesperson should cultivate relationships with purchasing agents, traffic persons, sales representatives, production supervisors, distributors and agents who influence the final decision of clients.

A salesperson should contact the company's customers from time to time with real concern, and they should inform the customers of new service or service improvement.

A salesperson should assist the client in getting a rate agreement and submit the request on behalf of the client. A salesperson should also conduct regular checks on cargo progress to ensure that the company meets its promises, and when it is not possible, they should contact the client and inform them.

It is the work of the salesperson to complete monthly customer reports and identify the business that each client is bringing.

A salesperson should create a good relationship with drivers and encourage openness. And finally, they should record their daily sales calls.

Dispatcher

Truck dispatchers might stay behind the scene, but they play a big role in the trucking industry. They ensure that the drivers have cargo and stick to their schedule. Dispatchers help drivers to focus on routes and deliver the cargo as promised.

A dispatcher must be a good speaker. This is because most of their work involves relaying information, and in a worst-case scenario, the driver may misunderstand them which can translate into losses for the company. Besides communicating with drivers, truck dispatchers also negotiate with vendors and talk to customers about cost-effective delivery means and the most efficient routes.

Chapter 18: Inspection and Maintenance

When you fail to maintain your truck, you won't be able to get more years of service from it. And so, you must always inspect and maintain your truck in the highest possible standards.

Preventive maintenance and regular inspection of trucks are useful in avoiding failures from occurring while the truck is moving on the road. Moreover, as you know, a failure is likely to lead to an accident. The funny thing is that most accidents that originate from mechanical failure are preventable. There are many guidelines for inspection and maintenance of commercial vehicles, and even the most consistent trucking companies may have challenges adhering to all the set rules.

Here are some tips for inspection and maintenance of your trucks:

Make your Maintenance Thorough

Always detail the repairs that your truck receives. If you find an emergent pattern of constant repairs, it may mean that you are not conducting thorough repairs. If you have to move from one mechanic to another in a short time span, it can make a serious dent in your money considering that these expenses will add up. And so, you have to invest in the best automotive services where your truck will be really inspected, and the proper services will be granted. It doesn't matter if the cost is high, as long as the problem will be dealt with conclusively.

Track Your Inspection and Maintenance Expenses

The FMCSA requires that you must record all the inspection, maintenance and repairs that have been done on your truck. This is important because, in the event of an accident, authorities can use this information to determine what the problem might be. Also, it is necessary to detail your inspection, maintenance, and repairs because it helps you track your expenses. Whenever you notice too many repairs for a similar problem, it might mean that you are not getting quality repairs services, and a truck that is often faulty poses a great deal of danger to other road users.

Monitor Wears and Tears

Not all accidents are caused by a lack of situational awareness on the part of the driver. Mechanical faults are also responsible for accidents. And in this case, mechanical faults happen because the owner hasn't invested in inspecting, repairing, and maintaining their trucks. One of the main triggers of mechanical faults is wear and tear. When the critical components of a truck suffer wear and tear, it stops the truck from functioning at its optimal level. This is likely to cause a breakdown while the truck is on the move, which may easily culminate in an accident.

Should Your Truck be Placed out of Service?

When a truck has exceeded certain limits, there is room for retiring it. The last thing you want is to be found operating a truck that is not supposed to be on the road. It would cost you a lot before that case is over. Actually, when you are caught operating a truck that is supposed to be off the road, it could be grounds enough for the FMCSA to cancel your operation license. So instead of risking your business, you had better retire your truck by first checking whether it matches the parameters.

Weigh the Effectiveness of Your Preventive Measures

You may have a scroll of maintenance, inspection and even safety measures, but the overriding question is whether they are effective. Some measures may be outdated, and others may not be suitable for your truck. And so, you need to work with experienced hands and safety coordinators to come up with maintenance, inspection and safety policies that are tailored to the needs of your truck company. Make sure that you develop policies and measures that are great at detecting defects. Also, ensure that you have a quick and effective response to defects.

Train Your Drivers

Your drivers should not just serve as robots that are responsible for driving your trucks, but it would help to enlighten them on the inspection, maintenance and safety policies as stipulated under the safety regulations. Train your drivers to become aware of a mechanical problem at the onset rather than wait for the defect to worsen. A small defect that could have been nipped if it were found early enough might balloon into a huge problem that could cost your company thousands of dollars. So you might want to have drivers who are keen on detecting small faults before they develop into huge mechanical problems.

Critical Parts

The maintenance and inspection should be conducted on the truck as a whole, but some parts need to be given special attention such as:

- Steering
- Brakes
- Couplers
- Wheels, and
- Suspension.

For instance, a defect in the rig could not be compared to a defect in the steering wheel. The rig can wait until you deliver the load and then you may fix it later. However, a defect in the steering wheel, brakes, couplers, wheel, and suspension should be rectified as soon as humanly possible, and this is because when such critical parts have defects, a road accident is usually in the cooking.

Chapter 19 : Promoting and Marketing your Freight Broker Business

Now that your business is up and running, you need to begin marketing your firm and your services. There are various ways of marketing your firm. Some ways are better and more effective depending on factors, such as your location and so on. One of the best pathways to success is heading where others are not. This means delving into opportunities that others are not aware of and perhaps even avoiding where everyone else is headed.

Here are some of the things that you can do.

Create a Business Website

Clients always want to know whom they are dealing with. Since you are unlikely to get to meet shippers and transporters in person, the next best platform is a business website.

Therefore, take the time to create a professional website. This website should be informative, user-friendly, and presentable. It should have your official business name, a logo, and a clear indication that you are a freight brokerage firm. You need to let your potential clients know about your services, any specialization, experience, and even accreditations.

Crucial information that your website should display is contact information. Make sure that you include your address, official business name, and other contact information, such as an email address and phone number. If you have an official mailing address, include this as well.

Apart from these details, let potential associates, clients, and the public know about your exceptional services that can be tailored for different shippers. Talk about all the positive attributes, including affordable rates, reliability, efficiency, and so on. You want people to know just how professional and excellent your services are. As soon as your website is ready, let it go live, then start the optimization process.

Website Optimization

Now that your website is up and running, no one will know about it unless it is properly optimized. Optimization is the process of getting your website to rank high on search engines whenever anyone conducts a relevant search.

For instance, when shippers search for a reliable freight broker using a search engine, you want your website to appear on the first page of the results. This is only possible with SEO optimization. SEO stands for search engine optimization. You can learn simple SEO techniques or let someone else optimize your website for you.

Write a Blog

A blog is a personal website where you write whatever you want. Since you are in a niche industry, you can write about freight services and inform your readers all about your work. Within a short time, you will be identified as an industry expert. People will reach out to you for an opinion and advice. Shippers will want to be associated with you. A blog is, therefore, a great way to market your firm and let others know about your professional services.

Blogging is easy, especially when you are writing about something that you are passionate about. You can write about your experience in the industry and any challenges you may have encountered. However, your readers mostly appreciate informative articles that are full of advice and detailed in explaining aspects. Take time to write carefully and write in a manner that is easy to understand.

Make sure that you engage your readers. Provide them with an interactive platform where they can ask questions or post comments. A blog is an excellent marketing strategy that is easy to implement and effective over the long-term.

How to Get Clients for your Business

Your aim now is to get out there and identify paying clients for your business. However, it is easier said than done. You need to know where to go to find shippers. There are plenty of places you can try. For instance, you can consider the numerous shipper databases or directories.

These directories are filled with manufacturers' addresses. Many of them use brokers to move their products. The only challenge is that hundreds of freight brokers use these directories trying to reach shippers. This means it is pretty challenging to secure steady clients. Also, you will be required to pay about $1,000 to access the database. To be successful, you will need to venture where others don't and avoid places where everyone goes.

Initial Client Interactions

Ideally, the best way to make contact with clients is via the Internet. Once an online connection has been established, you can then move on to the phone. Therefore, your first interaction with your client will be via phone. The problem is that, on most occasions, you will be redirected to voicemail.

If you leave a message, then your recipient will most likely not return your call. If you are unable to get a callback after three or four calls, you may want to move on to your next client. Most shippers are very busy individuals with a lot of work to do. If you come across a potential client, simply inquire whether they use freight brokers or not. If they do, then this is your chance to pitch your services. Take the chance to show how different you are from others. Have some confidence and speak well without stuttering. If your potential client has questions, be patient and listen to them. Then proceed to answer the questions as clearly as possible.

Remember that shippers have been in this business for a long time. They prefer talking to someone who knows what they are talking about. Therefore, do not beat about the bush; get straight to the point.

Diversification into Specialty Niches

The economy today is so immensely diversified that experts, such as freight brokers, can afford to specialize. When you start off, be open to engaging different shippers regardless of their loads. You do not want to lose out on any business.

Therefore, during the initial years, gain as many clients as you can and establish yourself. It is only much later that you will then decide to venture out into a specialty niche. Specialties can be very lucrative if you can be identified as an expert. This is because players in that niche will want to reach out to you, trusting that you will be able to deliver. Therefore, when the time comes, think about branching out into a specialty.

Although you will mostly be working from your home office, get some business cards. Business cards may sound outdated, but they come in handy when you are out and about. You will most likely bump into people who can help your business, so always carry some business cards. You may receive a call from a potential client when you least expect it. You can prepare some cards by yourself or pay a designer to do it for you.

How to Find Shippers

One of the biggest questions for new freight brokers is always where to find paying clients. This is an important question to ask, and the answer can determine the difference between a struggling brokerage and a successful one. The industry has developed immensely over the last decade or so. You can use freight broker software to carry out most tasks. However, the single most important aspect as a broker is finding clients for your firm.

As a freight broker and business owner, you want to find clients who will provide you with reliable, steady freight along lanes that you can cover. If you can find such clients and receive healthy margins, then you will be able to grow your business and live comfortably.

1. Consciously Observe the Brands around You

There are plenty of brands across the United States. They produce products that customers wish to purchase. Try and identify as many brands as you can in your neighborhood. If you wish to find shippers, then look at all the brands around you. Each brand is a potential client. The major brands produce products that are advertised and have to get to market.

2. Identify three new Business Contacts and Call them

Although it is never a good feeling, you should expect to lose a client occasionally. This is something that happens in every industry so do not be overly concerned. Due to this inevitable circumstance, it is smart to secure and call three different contacts daily. These contacts should be potential clients, so make sure that you contact them and see how it goes. Remember, if you only have one client, then your business will probably never get off the ground.

3. Do not Cold Call without Researching First

When you have a potential lead, don't call them before researching the company. If you call without any serious knowledge about a company, its operations or brands, then you could easily be dismissed, and they might not take your future calls. Research always impresses your caller.

4. Establish a Relationship

Once you make contact with a possible lead, try and establish a rapport. It is no secret that clients are more likely to buy from a friendly person than a total stranger. However, it's not easy to establish a rapport, especially when cold calling. The best way to do so is to talk about the client's lane or the volume they intend to move.

Other Ways of Finding Shippers

Observe other Companies in the Industry

If you have managed to get business with at least one company, then you should consider searching for their competitors. Find other companies in the same industry. You will probably come up with a number of companies. Research and find a way to contact them as they can be beneficial to you.

Observe A Company's other Branches

Suppose you already have a client in Fort Lauderdale, Florida. You will want to find out what other areas do the company operates in. If you notice areas where you have carrier relationships and the company has a presence, then this is a great place to source for additional business.

Check Out the Clients of your Client

You should also take a closer look at the clients of your client. Most major companies have many operations across different locations. If you deliver goods to one destination for further processing, then those goods will still have to get to another destination. Think about providing transport to that other destination. Since you are already a trusted partner, you could easily get additional business.

Co-Brokering and Double Brokering

For a long time, people have confused co-brokering with double brokering. However, there is a difference between the two. It is important to understand the difference because one is legal and one is risky:

Co-brokering: This is where you, the freight broker, accept a load from your client and then hand it to another broker to process and arrange transportation. It is legal and is acceptable.

Double brokering: This is the situation where a carrier accepts to transport goods on behalf of a client but then brokers a transportation deal with another company to transport the goods. In this case, the load has been double brokered.

Double brokering does not have any benefits; only downsides. It is also not allowed. On the other hand, co-brokering is acceptable and allowed. However, the original agreement between the parties sometimes specifies that either practice is not allowed.

Powerful Lead Generation Tips for Freight Brokers

1. Begin with people you know well or your current social circle. Make professional looking business cards and brochures and let them know you've launched a new freight brokering business. Ask your social contacts, friends, acquaintances and distant family members about the organizations they are employed with. You never know, these firms may need shipping services and may come knocking on your door. While most zealous startup founders chase slick lead generation techniques, most ignore the power of tapping into your own backyard for business. Get a breakthrough into an industry through your initial contacts, and later build on it by targeting other firms in the same field/industry.

2. I always advice new freight brokering professionals and companies to keep a notepad and paper handy in their vehicle for jotting down the names of companies they spot while travelling. Mention the name of the company, prominent landmarks, any contact information or anything else of special mention which can come handy in the rapport building process. You may note special information like they are the city's biggest paper manufacturers or a fast food chain with the largest turnover in town. Get the idea? Anything notable and striking about the organization will do.

3. Build a clean and awesome reputation so you get plenty of referrals from existing customers. Your existing customers are the best evangelists for your freight brokerage firm. When word

spreads through the industry about your professional and prompt services, other companies may want to try your services too. Let us say a company had to ship their consignment somewhere and at the last minute, trucks weren't available. The first thing those companies will do is check with their contacts if any alternate trucking companies or trucks are available. If you have a good reputation in the market, the contacts or other companies in the industry who've received satisfactory services from you will recommend your name to the stranded companies. This can give you plenty of referral leads. In fact, I'll go a step ahead and urge you ask companies you've served well for referrals.

After serving a company, you can give them a feedback form or actively ask them for feedback along with names of companies they think can benefit from your services. You'll be surprised at the number of leads you generate through existing customers. While talking to the new prospective customer or company, you can mention that their contact xyz referred them to you since their contact thought they'd (the referred companies) will benefit from your services. Also companies you've shipped to. Avoid contacting them before successfully completing the consignment. It is easier to approach companies when you have some success to show them.

4. Grab plenty of leads on Thomasnet.com, Begin contact the customers on the Thomas.net database. There are literally thousands of prospects to target there. If you are uncomfortable with the prospect of picking from a random database, begin with an industry that you are familiar with. This will help you start and progress with greater confidence. You may have worked in a specific industry earlier, and may have a good working understanding of the sector. Start with it, and move on from there to cold calling other industries.

5. Research your drop off destination for consignments. Do a bit of research on the drop destination of your present load lot. Chances

are there may be loads to be shipped from there. Plus, you'll probably be able to offer a more competitive price since you already have the transport logistics ready at the destination and don't have to organize any special transportation. To make the most of the trip to the destination, connect companies that may need moving consignment from there and offer them a reduced price. This way you'll optimize your resources.

Also, call the companies where your current load is being dropped off and ask beforehand if they have any loads that need to be picked up since you will anyway be having transportation ready after dropping off the consignment to them. You won't always hit jackpot using this method. However, at times, these companies may have their own load to drop off, where you can quickly seize the opportunity by offering them reduced shipping rates. Stay persistent when approaching these companies. They may not have anything for you at first. However, if you persist, they may just give you a one off order and then turn it into regular business if they are satisfied with your services.

6. Include a referral bonus at the end of every mail you send. As a freight broker, you send plenty of emails to prospects as well as non-prospects (who can very well be converted into prospects). View every mail you send as an opportunity to refer someone who needs your services to you. Offer what it presently costs, including your time and money to get a new customer. Is it worth it, you ask? Do the calculations yourself. Incentivize your current network to give yourself better business. You may spend some money initially on these referrals however the value of new customers (who may in turn bring new customers or repeat purchases) is tremendous. This is how you go your business.

7. Identify other shipping destinations within the same company. Say you've established a good working relationship with the shipping in charge of the shipping plant of the main company. However, the main company many have plenty of other locations

across the country. These may also happen to areas where you've established carrier relationships. Use your networking and relationship building skills (hallmark of a good freight broker) to get your contacts to introduce you to shipping managers of different locations of the same firm. Get word of mouth referrals.

Ensure that you don't straight off ask your contacts for connections introductions. Be a little discreet and use your discretion. You'll need to do some fishing for on the phone and email to prequalify leads. Get a feel of your contact's rapport shipping managers of other locations.

You'll also want to feel out what your contact knows about the arrangements at the shipping location you would like to start getting business from. One of the best ways to establish connections is to pull out performance statistics from freight broker software, and paste them on a sheet out together by a professional. Find designers of Fiverr or Upwork at a reasonable price.

Conclusion

Before you can start operations, you will need a commercial driver's license and receive relevant training. It is absolutely necessary to receive training as it sets the driver on the path to success.

A good business plan should estimate revenue and expenses; thus, it should be both realistic and ambitious. It takes an experienced hand to arrive at conclusions concerning the economic viability of a trucking company, and so, if you are new to this industry, you might want to work with a person who is experienced.

The sole proprietorship may give you all the control, but it is not a prudent economic decision. This is because it opens up your personal assets to vulnerabilities. The best business structure is the one that grants you a limited liability, considering that you will need financing from money lending institutions.

One of the challenges of running a Freight Broker Business is managing your expenses. There is a lot of stuff that needs to be paid for on regular terms, for example, repairs, maintenance, and operational costs. Thanks to technology, you can use management software that tracks your company's expenses and helps you to manage the fleet under one platform.

You must take care that you observe the rules and regulations. The Freight Broker Business is highly regulated. Truckers are held to very high standards because of the sensitive nature of their jobs. Failure to comply might see your operating license suspended and, in worse cases, you might be banned from engaging in further business within the industry.

Made in the USA
Columbia, SC
06 October 2020